# Time Travel Invasion

## By

## Rob Shelsky

TIME TRAVEL INVASION

PUBLISHED BY: GKRS Publications

ISBN-13:978-1533588111

ISBN-10:1533588112

Copyright © 2016

By

Rob Shelsky

All rights reserved. Without limiting the rights under copyright reserved above, no part of this publication may be reproduced, stored in or introduced into a retrieval system, or transmitted, in any form, or by any means (electronic, mechanical, photocopying, recording, printing or otherwise) without the prior written permission of both the copyright owner and the above publisher of this book.

This is a work of nonfiction. The author acknowledges the trademarked status and trademark owners of various products referenced in this work of nonfiction, which have been used without permission. The publication/use of these trademarks is not authorized, associated with, or sponsored by the trademark owners.

**Edition License Notes:**

This ebook is licensed through GKRS Publications for your personal enjoyment only. This ebook may not be resold or given away to other people. If you would like to share this book with another person, please purchase an additional copy for each person you share it with. If you're reading this book and did not purchase it, or it was not purchased for your use only, then you should purchase your own copy. Thank you for respecting the author's work.

\* \* \* \* \*

## OTHER BOOKS BY ROB SHELSKY:

*DARKER SIDE OF THE MOON "They" Are Watching Us!* A nonfiction book on the dangers UFOs present. *Ancient Alien Empire Megalithia, Mysteries of Time Travel: 35 Cases of Time Travel Intrusion, Invader Moon, Deadly UFOS And The Disappeared, For The Moon Is Hollow And Aliens Rule The Sky,* and *Mysteries Of Mothman,* all available at: Amazon.com, in Kindle or print, and Smashwords.com for all other ebook formats. Available in print at CreateSpace.com, Amazon.com.

\* \* \* \* \*

*A VERY SPECIAL DEDICATION*
TO
*A VERY SPECIAL PERSON*
~ Diane Powell ~
A Friend When In Need, Indeed!
True In The Past, True In The Present
And Certain To Be True In The Future.
Lifelong Friends Are Rare, So I Treasure
Her.


ALSO DEDICATED
*IN MEMORIAM*
TO
~ *GEORGE A. KEMPLAND* ~
Wherever You Are Now, George,
May You Always Be Happy,
At Peace, And Enjoying Yourself.
I Hope I May Get To See You Again…
Somewhen.

# CONTENTS

| | |
|---|---|
| INTRODUCTION | 1 |
| CHAPTER 1 | 7 |
| CHAPTER 2 | 14 |
| CHAPTER 3 | 28 |
| CHAPTER 4 | 49 |
| CHAPTER 5 | 60 |
| CHAPTER 6 | 81 |
| CHAPTER 7 | 92 |
| CHAPTER 8 | 105 |
| CHAPTER 9 | 124 |
| CHAPTER 10 | 130 |
| CHAPTER 11 | 138 |
| CHAPTER 12 | 151 |
| CHAPTER 13 | 157 |
| CHAPTER 14 | 165 |
| CHAPTER 15 | 179 |
| CHAPTER 16 | 193 |
| CHAPTER 17 | 209 |
| CHAPTER 18 | 218 |
| CHAPTER 19 | 232 |
| CHAPTER 20 | 238 |
| CHAPTER 21 | 243 |
| CHAPTER 22 | 250 |
| CHAPTER 23 | 258 |
| CONCLUSION | 263 |
| ABOUT THE AUTHOR | 273 |
| REFERENCES | 275 |

# INTRODUCTION

*"Time travel used to be thought of as just science fiction, but Einstein's general theory of relativity allows for the possibility that we could warp space-time so much that you could go off in a rocket and return before you set out."*

— Stephen Hawking

**Time Travel Is Real!** This statement is obviously a bold one. The idea time travel might even be possible goes contrary to what the majority of scientists and researchers believed even just a few years ago, or perhaps, would ever contemplate saying even now. Likewise, many lay people would consider the possibility of time travel an incredible one.

Yet, considerable evidence has accrued over the past several years to back the idea of time travel being a very real possibility. For some researchers, time travel might even be a ***distinct probability***! A surprising thing for them to say, certainly, but so some have. For this reason, I've written this book, because of this sea change among some researchers regarding the idea of time travel, and because of other evidence that has been accumulating, as well.

This book not only will discuss the evidence supporting time travel being possible and real, but also intends to go much further with the idea of time travel, what it means for us. For example, it is the contention of some that:

**Time Travel Has Been Done Already!** This is an equally bold statement as the others and again, many upon first reading this will consider the idea an absurd one…but perhaps, only at first.

Again, this book will attempt to show evidence why the author thinks the idea of time travel already is a probable reality, and not just some bizarre notion of a fringe element or "oddball" group. As with the first statement in this introduction, evidence from a variety of sources will back this theory.

**Time Travelers, Invaders From The Future Or "Elsewhere," Are Real.** This idea would natural follow the other two statements. If time travel is real, then we must have had invaders from the future, or "elsewhere" (and we will discuss that idea further later on) who have come into the past and interfered with our timeline. The consequences for us if this is true are incredible.

Could someone be interfering with our history, our present, and so altering the natural course of events of our future? Could such interference simply cause people to have never been born that otherwise would have, and so have not only ceased to exist, but never have been at all? This is a chilling conclusion. Again, we will discuss one in depth here in *Time Travel Invasion*.

**Is Our Universe The Real One?** This question, at first glance, may not seem as if it relates to the topic of time travel at all, but it most definitely does as will be shown later on. A hypothesis of some physicists and cosmologists, and even a number of quantum physics experts, is the idea our universe might not be the "real one."

If our universe proves not to be, then as to what is possible and is not with regard to time travel is a matter open for some considerable speculation. In other words, when it comes to time travel, all bets just might be off.

Of course, even if this book supplies strong support for the idea time travel is an actual reality and has been done already, there are several big questions (among many lesser ones) remaining, and these are:

**Just Who Is Doing The Time Traveling?** Are aliens perpetrating the fouling of our timeline by interjecting themselves into it for some hidden purpose? Alternatively, is it our future selves coming to the past, or even "someone" else? There are other possible questions, as well. For instance, what if it is someone "outside" our universe doing this? If so, are we the victims of some "others" who might have created us for their own purposes? If so, what might those purposes be?

**Why Is Time Travel Happening?** If time travel is real and it does seem to be (and yes, once again, evidence will be supplied to support this contention), and has been done, then of course we need to know why it is being done. More specifically, we also need to know what it means to us, as individuals, and as a society. What are the consequences for us?

**Is Someone Manipulating Our Timeline?** If so, for what ultimate purpose? What do "they have in mind for us? Furthermore, what are the ramifications for us as individuals? Are we in any sort of danger? Could we be "instantly wiped out" as some science fiction books and movies suggest when our timeline is altered?

Alternatively, is "someone" trying to save us by altering events? Worse, are they trying ultimately to destroy us at some point in our future by manipulating what are already past events for them, and somehow changing them to their liking in "their" present? The matter might be simpler. Perhaps someone is just performing some weird experiment with us?

If any of this is true, we desperately then need to know who is doing such things. Only then can we assign possible motivations to whoever might be doing temporal (time) engineering in our timeline.

Then, we might figure out what the alterations are and what their outcomes might be. Again, we need to know the answers to these questions if only for our own sakes.

**Is There Something More To All This Than We Can Ever Realize, Something More Profound And Stunning Than We Might Have Even Thought Possible?** As we shall see later on, this last could well be the case, as well. Evidence that supports this idea as a possible real one is also available, and we will discussed it here in this book.

How could any of us hope to determine answers to any of these questions? Well, we can start by taking them one at a time, looking at the available evidence to support each of them, and so delve into the likelihood of any of the possible answers being the more likely correct ones.

There are many aspects to the whole idea of time travel, as one can see, and many side issues, complications, and potential problems, as well. *Time Travel Invasion* will attempt to provide an in-depth look at all of this and provide evidence to back the main contentions of this book. Again, it is the author's intention to reach some kind of answers to the questions asked in this introduction. There are many topics to cover. Among them are:

—Is Time Travel Real?

—Has Time Travel Been Accomplished?

—Who Is Doing The Time Traveling?

—Why Are "They" Doing Time Traveling?

—Is Our Timeline Being Manipulated?

—What Would Be The Purpose of Manipulation Of Our Timeline?

—Evidence For The Idea Of Time Travel.

—Backward Time Travel.

— Is Time Travel A "One-Way Street?"

— Can We Be Both Dead And Alive At The Same Time?

— A Quantum Drum.

— Sideways Time Travel.

— Memories of Other Timelines?

— The Mandela Effect.

— Binary Code In The Basic Fabric Of Our Universe?

— Evidence For Time Travelers.

— Are "Black-Eyed Children" More Evidence of Time Travelers?

— Project Pegasus.

— Deciphering The Future.

— Quantum Weirdness and the "Nonlocality" of Space-Time.

— Is Our Universe The "Real One?"

— Pulsar Quakes And What They Might Mean For Time Travel

— Time "Glitches?" What's The Connection?

— Are We In Danger From Time Travel Invasion?

— A Universe Of Games?

— The Consequences For Us.

There are more topics, as well. However, please note, **none** of these subjects will involve overly complicated explanations, ones that are hard to understand.

This book is not written to discuss in-depth the laws of physics and the mathematical mechanics of time travel. Rather, the author writes in an easy-going style, just so as not to be confusing or difficult.

Author Rob Shelsky feels it is the point that is important here, and not the mathematical details, although he does cite references for them for those who might want to follow up on them. Therefore, he handles the whole subject of time travel and the various aspects of it in a natural and unaffected way.

So if you would like to know more about the idea of time travel being real, having already occurred, and if we are the victims of *Time Travel Invasion,* or what the repercussions might be for us, please read on.

# CHAPTER 1

## How Do We Find Proof Of Time Travel?

*"The bottom line is that time travel is allowed by the laws of physics."*

—Brian Greene,

**Theoretical and String Theory Physicist**

If time travel is real and, how do we go about finding proof of this fact? Well, the truth is, that's not so easy a thing to do. After all, if someone has changed time, then for us who came after the point of that change in the timeline, any such alterations would seem a normal part of our history. The changes have always been there and something that just happened in our past. Such a time alteration would be, therefore, a seemingly "natural" part of our history and so nothing out of the ordinary. In other words, we only know the way things have now happened for us, not the way they might have happened before, or been before such alterations in our timeline might have occurred.

For instance, the fact Richard Nixon was never assassinated is just a normal part of our history. If someone had assassinated him, and our timeline then had been changed after the fact so it had never occurred, how could we possibly know this?

We could only know the current version of our history, not possible ones that might have once existed and then been changed and so are no more. For that matter, how could we even know how many times such a thing might have occurred? History books that might have once said President Nixon was assassinated, or assassinated later in his term, now would not say that, but instead give a history of his term in office (as they now do) until his resignation.

So once more, how can we know if time travel is happening? Yes, it would be far easier if people from the future showed up in shiny silver suits with all sorts of marvelous inventions and told us this flat out, that they were from the future. However, let's be real here; such a thing is very unlikely to happen and for a variety of reasons.

Anyone intent on changing history to achieve some desired new outcome just isn't going to shout what they are doing from the rooftops to us. That, in itself, might adversely change things for them.

No, they would probably do whatever they are doing in quiet, with a minimum of fuss, so as not to interfere with their desired results by any such extra and accidental manipulations of our timeline. Consequently, we can't expect such obvious evidence for time travel. Such a thing just wouldn't be likely.

Does this then make determining if there has been time travel impossible to do? No, certainly not, but it does make it harder for us to do. Still, there are other ways we can approach the idea of time travel, and utilize different methods of finding evidence for it, and for time travelers. We've done it before with other things.

Case in point; for example, just as astronomers have to find evidence for the existence of black holes through secondary means, because black holes themselves, by their very nature, are invisible to us, so must we do the same with trying to find time travelers. If we can't spot them outright, maybe we can know them by their actions in one way or another, just as scientists do with black holes. Perhaps there is evidence of this sort available to us time-travel hunters?

Of course, the best sort of evidence is that which is derived from multiple sources and different types of sources, and not just one. These pieces of evidence would then help support and corroborate each other. Therefore, what types of evidence are we talking about here?

Well, stories of time travel encounters by various people are great, but on their own, they don't prove that time travel is happening. They simply aren't enough evidence in and of themselves.

Nevertheless, they still do aid the idea, but again on their own, they just aren't enough for most scientists to consider them as a confirmation of the idea time travel is real. Although, if we have many such tales from reliable witnesses, then more credence definitely can apply to the idea time travel is not only real, but is happening.

Even so, we still need other sources for the idea of time travel being an actuality, as well. If we have these extra types of evidence, we then have a stronger and better foundation.

Such additional evidence combined with witness accounts then create a "body of evidence" we can most likely rely upon. The concept of time travel would then have a far stronger basis on which to stand, rather than relying solely on anecdotal evidence. However, are there such additional forms of evidence we can use?

Luckily, for us here, there does seem to be. We do have multiple sorts of evidence available to us. They include, but are not limited to:

1. **Strange, Seemingly Out-Of-Place Occurrences In History.** Besides just relying on the stories of witnesses, however reliable, we can also look for extraordinary occurrences in our history, unaccountable events that just don't seem to fit any other explanation than time travel, and so seem bizarrely out of place otherwise. Other authors have done this, as I have with books on ancient aliens, principally to show extraterrestrials have visited us in the past. The principle should then also work for time travel if we can find such evidence for it, too.

However, just having Christopher Columbus seeing strange lights appear in the skies of our world in 1492 (and according to his own log, he did), for example, isn't enough to prove time travel is real, although it might well lend credence to the idea of extraterrestrials really existing and having done so for a long time.

To show time travel is involved, we have to be able to go even further. We need something more than just having the appearance of such lights or UFOs somehow having taken place at a critical historical moment, and in a crucial location and time.

Besides just appearing throughout our history, the objects then have to have **directly acted to intervene** to change the course of history as it might have unfolded otherwise if there had been no such intervention. Such intrusions of UFOs would then be purposeful to change the timeline. They would have been in order to alter our timeline at critical junctures. This is just one example of such a type of evidence.

**2. Actual Cases Of People Reporting Time Travel Or Time Travelers.** Again, a few stories of witnesses and victims of time travel or time travelers is helpful, but just not enough. Either we have to have more solid evidence involved, or we have to have a lot of these stories and from reputable sources! The sheer numbers of such tales would then act to lend some better credence to the idea of time travel/travelers.

The good news is we do have such stories and many are from impeccable sources. There are a lot more of these tales than you might think, as well. Moreover, we do have some "hard" evidence to go along with some of these tales, interwoven with them.

Therefore, this is yet another way to prove the fact of time travel being real and actually happening. If enough people are reporting the fact of beings coming from a future or past time to visit and/or interact with them, and their stories seem credible enough, preferably with some sort of confirming hard evidence involved, then we can reasonably conclude time travel interference is taking place. Again, the more of these people with such stories there are, the more likely this acts as a reliable form of evidence in its own right.

**3. "Hard" Evidence Of Time Travel.** Another and much sought after type of evidence is so-called "hard" evidence. This is evidence that is considered solid, being either items left behind by time travelers, evidence in the form of old unretouched photographs, movies, etc., showing major inconsistencies, anachronisms (things that are out of place for the time the photo was taken, for example).

Also real objects discovered in archeology that just shouldn't be where they are found would be evidence. These last would be things that just don't fit the time in which people discovered them.

Of course, getting one's hands on a working time machine would be the ultimate proof, but let's be honest; this just isn't very likely to happen. Still, in lieu of that, other things, as described in the above paragraphs would certainly go a long way to verifying time travel being real, that there are time travelers, and events in our timeline just might be subject to changes. To prove this to any degree that's what we need to concentrate on here, just such types of evidence.

**4. Other Forms Of Proof That Time Travel Exists Or Can Exist.** We can determine other ways if time travel is real, as well. For instance, examples of this type of evidence would be as with the laws of physics and/or related scientific evidence that allows for, or even attests to the fact of the reality of time travel.

If science says traveling through time is possible, if researchers are working on various aspects of time travel because of this fact, then this forms yet another type of evidence for time travel being real. In other words, if it is possible and we are working on it now, then it is likely people in the future would do the same and so may have already accomplished their goals in that regard.

Also, if enough people have similar memories of something being different than it now is that too, could constitute supporting evidence of the idea of time travel. In other words, if many people "remember" something being one way, but history is now different from that, then perhaps a change has taken place, one these people have not subsequently forgotten. This is a real phenomenon, by the way, and often goes by the term, "the Mandela Effect." We will cover this effect in more depth later on in this book.

**Conclusion:** So here we have a number of types of evidence we might use for determining if time travel is possible, if it is real, and it if has, in fact, already been done. The more types of such information we have, the stronger is our case that time travel is real, and "somebody" is interfering with our timeline.

Now, we simply have to look for such types of evidence and if finding them, we can then determine the likelihood if time travel is real and has actually taken place. Up front, I can say there is such evidence. Furthermore, it is amazing just how much evidence there is!

We'll start with the last point, Number 4 above, **Other Forms Of Proof**, first, and specifically any evidence that currently science supports the idea of time travel. We will get to the remaining types of evidence just a bit later on.

# CHAPTER 2

## Is Time Travel Possible With Current Scientific Theories?

*"Even if it turns out that time travel is impossible, it is important that we understand why it is impossible."*

— Stephen Hawking

**Time Travel Is Possible According To Science.** That's the short answer to the question in this chapter heading. Time travel is possible within the laws of physics, as we understand them right now, although it would be difficult to do such travel to any meaningful extent with our current level of technology. Again, time travel is possible with the laws of physics right now. Moreover, there are a number of different ways to accomplish such temporal travel.

We will not go into too many details on the various ways such possible methods of time travel can occur, but we do need to take a quick glance at each of them, just to set the stage for what comes after in the way of evidence.

There is one proven method of time travel already, a way we already do it see. Farther on in this book, we will discuss this topic. Yet and despite this and the fact that not only physics in general, but the great Albert Einstein himself believed time travel was theoretically possible, for many, the idea of time travel is viewed with just downright loathing.

These people claim such travel is against the laws of physics (it's not, as we shall see) and even against the very structural nature of the universe itself and so therefore, simply can't be done.

Rather than saying this to you, such people would instead tell you that time travel is just *"highly unlikely."* They simply won't give you a flat, *"no, time travel is impossible,"* even though they may believe this.

There is a reason for this equivocation. Scientists of today have learned the hard way to avoid such phrases as "impossible" and "never will happen." How did this state of affairs come about? Well there are many examples of why, but here's just one quick instance, again, one of many is an illustration of what we deal with in so-called objective science:

As strange, as it may seem and not so very long ago, less than a century in fact, many reputable scientists around the world believed that rockets couldn't work in space. Such a thing was impossible they said, because "there was no air" for the rocket's exhaust to push against to propel it forward. Some of these scientists, even including an engineer with a long and great reputation, adhered to this idea, that travel in space by a rocket ship was impossible. It was, according to them, and despite Newton's Three Laws of Motion, against the laws of physics.

This position and attitude later caused some major embarrassment for those who thought this. Case in point, in 2009, *The New York Times* printed a retraction of a January 13, 1920, full-page editorial. In part, the editorial had said:

"*That professor Goddard [referring to rocket scientist, [Robert Goddard], with his 'chair' in Clark college and the countenancing of the Smithsonian Institution, does not know the relation of action to reaction, and of the need to have something better than a vacuum against which to react -- to say that would be absurd. Of course he only seems to lack the knowledge ladled out daily in high schools.*" **[Emphasis added.]**

Rather a scathing rebuke, isn't it? The article virtually called Robert Goddard a simpleton in this regard for believing rockets could travel through space. The article rather bluntly implied the noted professor was basically dumber than a rug, and should know a reaction requires something to push against in order to work, which the vacuum of space does not provide, being empty.

Of course, *The New York Times* editorial was very wrong as we now all know. The editorial ignored Isaac Newton's Third Law of Motion, no less. This law simply states that "for every action there is an equal and opposite reaction."

Newton didn't add the condition: "but it doesn't work in space because there is nothing for the reaction to react against." Nor did he add any other conditions, either. The Third Law of Motion was elegant in its sheer simplicity.

What else did the retraction say besides repeating the above faulty editorial information? Well, it admitted NASA was right (among many others) after all, and that *The New York Times* was indeed, completely wrong in every respect. Rockets did work in the vacuum of space and so space travel was actually possible, and indeed, had been accomplished any number of times already by the time of the printing of the retraction. They were understandably a little slow; it seems, in getting around to that part of it.

Therefore, these days, because of many events like the above, scientists and the rest of us have learned to be very careful whenever we make statements about something being impossible. In fact, many researchers now say, if only to cover themselves for later on, that almost "anything is possible until proven to be otherwise."

There is another reason why they try to avoid such rigid statements. That is, technology. Technology has a way of making liars of us all by making the impossible become quite possible, and far more swiftly than we once thought likely. Consequently, it would seem time travel, at least in public and according to most scientists, may be unlikely, but perhaps, just perhaps, is not actually impossible. In others words, they admit, if reluctantly, such travel just might be conceivable. Admittedly, their statements in this regard often only come under a certain duress...

The truth is they have even more reason not to be sure, whether time travel is impossible and they are good ones. As previously mentioned, even in today's understanding of physics, time travel does seem to be achievable. Furthermore, perhaps such travel is possible in not just one, but in several different ways. Thus, before we launch into all the other aspects of the whole question of time travel being real, we should just take a brief look at these, first:

**1. Einstein's Special Theory of Relativity Allows For Time Travel.** We won't dwell on this point long, because most people are now well aware of this particular item. However, around 1905, the unsurpassed genius, Albert Einstein, formulated his Special Theory of Relativity and it allowed certain things not only to be possible, but also to actually work.

**a. Traveling Forward In Time.** This is already an actual proven method of time travel, because in part, Einstein's theory stated that, as one article put it, "Travelling *forwards in time is surprisingly easy.*" (See *"References"* for links to more in-depth articles on this.) As it turns out, it truly is easy! Moreover, we've actually done it and we do it constantly.

According to Einstein, time moves at different rates depending on the speed or velocity of the object involved. Simply put, the faster the person(s) or object moves, the closer it gets to the speed of light, and so the slower time passes for them from the point of view of the outside observer. Of course, for the person or vehicle actually involved, time appears to pass at a normal rate. However, for the observer watching them, they see time apparently slowing for the speeding person or object they are viewing.

The famous "twin paradox" is a great example of this and easy to understand. One twin boards a spaceship and sets off into space at close to the speed of light. The other stays on Earth. The twin in the spaceship returns just a few years later in his/her time. However, for the one left on Earth, decades have already passed. The twin left on Earth has grown old in the meantime. Therefore, for the twin in the spaceship, s/he has for all practical purposes, traveled in time, has moved decades into Earth's future, and after having only traveled for a few years of their time. Again, time travel into the future is, to reiterate, *"Surprisingly easy."* Except, of course, for the fact it is hard to go that close to the speed of light with current technology.

Even so, we know this type of time travel to be true for a certainty. Experiment after experiment has confirmed the fact that Einstein's Special Theory of Relativity is real and it works without fail every time in this regard. Atomic clocks placed in orbital vehicles, those moving around the Earth faster than we move here on Earth, show that time for them has slowed compared to atomic clocks "twinned" with them but left here on Earth.

Additionally, our entire GPS satellite system constantly has to compensate for this "time slowdown" of things moving faster in orbit. This compensation is in order for the GPS tracking system devices we use here on Earth to stay correct. Otherwise, our location devices, whether in phones, computers, or whatever, would increase in error with every passing hour to the point where they would be so far off, they would be useless in short order. So constant automatic recalibrating of the system is necessary for the atomic clocks to compensate for the 38 microseconds they would otherwise gain every single day.

Without such compensation, one wouldn't be able to pinpoint anything on a GPS map with any accuracy at all. The results would be off by a number of miles and very quickly. The atomic clocks must be accurate to within 30 nanoseconds (30 billionths of a second), at least, for the GPS system to maintain its present wonderful accuracy.

This phenomenon proves the point; traveling "forward" in time using this method not only works, but also works well, and is being accomplished every hour of every day. Even so, this isn't really a good method of time travel, since the persons traveling faster aboard a spaceship, for instance, could not return to their own time. Whatever time they would travel forward to, is where they must remain. There is no coming back, no way to reverse with this means of travel. Therefore, such a time traveller wouldn't just be giving the future a brief visit. They'd be stuck there! There would be no going back.

Just in case you are wondering, one can't go faster than the speed of light or so current physics and Einstein tells us. Breaking the speed of light seems forbidden. Scientists consider the speed of light to be a universal constant, that is, unchangeable and unsurpassable. Nothing we know of, not energy or any form of matter, anything with "mass" to it, can break this speed barrier.

Furthermore, just in case you also may be wondering, the speed of light, precisely, is 299,792,458 meters per second, or a little less precisely, about 186,000 miles per second. That's just about 7-1/2 times around the Earth in one second. If you wish to know more about the speed of light, there is a link listed under the *"References"* section at the end of this book.

**b. Wormholes.** Another part of Einstein's Special Relativity Theory allows for the existence of wormholes. If wormholes exist, and we have no reason to believe they don't, since Einstein seems to have been consistently correct in his theory in all other matters so far, then two wormholes, separated and moving, would allow one to travel through them and thus also through time. The person, if they entered the one wormhole (connected to the other) would emerge not only in a different location in the universe, but also in a different time, as well. However, it is theoretically possible they will also emerge into another universe entirely. Accordingly, this is probably not a reliable method of time travel. That is, unless we can come up with some way to figure out in advance where, exactly, the wormholes would take us.

The only problem with this scenario, according to some physicists, including Kip Thorne, a theoretical researcher, is that such time-travel wormholes would collapse immediately upon formation. Thus, this collapse would "naturally" prevent time travel. Nevertheless, if we could use something called "negative energy" to maintain the opening of the wormhole, then time travel would be possible. One could then enter the hole and so emerge again from the other end one.

Strangely, we do have strong evidence that negative energy exists. Quantum Theory shows this with the so-called Casimir Effect in experiments that always work without fail. We won't go into details on this, since for our purposes it is unnecessary in order to prove our point, but the experiment does show negative energy definitely comes into play. There are a couple of other types of negative energy, as well. One of these is "virtual" negative-energy particles, ones created because of Hawking Radiation emanating from black holes.

Again, for our purposes here, it isn't necessary to go into the details of the exact nature of this type of negative energy. It is enough for us to know that negative energy exists and so perhaps we could keep a time-travel, wormhole mouth open. Again, if you would like more in-depth information on these types of energy in easy-to-read formats, please see the links under the *"References"* section at the end of this book.

Furthermore, we have not discussed "dark energy" here, since not enough is known about its nature, really (hence, the term "dark energy," because it's pretty much an unknown), but this energy could have strong implications for time travel, as well. Exactly what they might be is also unknown at this point.

Nevertheless, with regard to wormholes, an important thing to note here about possible time-travel with them is that one cannot go back in time before a wormhole exists. That would be rather like traveling in a car before it was built or started its journey. Therefore, there are limits to how far back in time one could go using such a method.

**2. Rotating Black Holes And Time Travel.** A rotating black hole, if orbited closely, in theory should propel the traveler forward in time. Again, the person doing the traveling would have to do so at a very high speed, close to the speed of light in order to travel an appreciable distance through time, so this method has its problems, as well. We simply would not be able to achieve such speeds with our current methods of propulsion. Chemical-based rockets, as most of our rockets now are, would be woefully inadequate in this regard and in many other respects, as well.

**3. Kerr Black Holes.** Another type of black hole might also allow for time travel, a so-called Kerr Black Hole. These are theoretical, but mathematically they could well exist. Of course, we once thought black holes of any sort were impossible, and could only exist mathematically, as well, but we were obviously wrong about that one! We know now that black holes definitely exist.

So Kerr Black Holes might well exist, too, and if they do, time travel through them (perhaps even to other universes, as well) could be possible without the traveler being crushed to death by the enormous gravity well of a standard black hole's singularity. We would simply fly through such a black hole without problems. Again, we don't need the specifics of the mechanics of this here. We only need to know the fact such Kerr Black Holes would allow for time travel, and could well exist. In any case, this would constitute another possible method of time travel.

Again, black holes do exist and if orbited under the right circumstances could allow time travel. One faction in the scientific community even argues that orbiting a rotating black hole in reverse could throw one back in time. However, as with the wormholes, one couldn't go back further in time than the black hole existed. Yet, some black holes are very old; indeed, there are some billions of years in age. They formed near the very start of the universe. So maybe, it's just a matter of finding one of those to use as a time travel device.

**4. Physics "Dirty Little Secret."** As described by some physicists, the science of physics has a *"dirty little secret."* By this, they mean there is something odd about equations they use in physics and that is they work either way, forward or backward!

In other words, they don't need "cause and effect" to work in the normal way. Nothing has to cause an effect. Rather, the reverse can be true, effect can come first and then the cause. By this, we mean that something must first happen and then an effect follows, as with tipping over a pot of boiling water on one's arm by mistake (the cause) and the (effect) the arm then scalded. In our present world of time as we think of it, as we know it, the cause always has to come first, and then followed by the effect. For instance, one couldn't feel the burn of boiling water before one has accidentally poured it onto one's arm, right?

However, again in physics with regard to the mathematical equations they use, cause and effect simply don't matter. The formulas work just as well in either direction, no matter which comes first, whether cause or effect! **This mean that for physics, the flow of time as we think of it simply doesn't matter!**

**5. Professor "Stirs" Space-Time To Build Time Machine.** Professor Ronald Lawrence "Ron" Mallett is a theoretical physicist. In today's world of physics, he is well known for his position on the idea of time travel being real. Professor Mallett has long been seriously interested in building a time machine. He is currently experimenting on just such a thing, at least a very basic prototype. Having lost his father when the man was still very young, the physicist, as a boy, dreamed of such a machine in which he could travel back in time and save his dad. This, then, became a lifelong goal, somehow to create such a time machine.

Additionally, this dream was instrumental in him even becoming a physicist, so strong was this desire, as mentioned on the television show, *This American Life*. Professor Mallet believes that Einstein's Special Theory allows space-time to be "stirred" in effect, by using a rotating beam of a laser, much as one might stir a cup of coffee with a plastic stirrer.

Again, this method of time travel is currently under experimentation. They have not yet released the preliminary results. Even so, it is the physicist's theory that if done properly, time, or spacetime, can be "curved" enough by this stirring to loop back on itself, just as coffee in a cup can be stirred until it creates a small whirlpool. Professor Mallet believes this can happen to the point where someone actually could go back in time, say to the moment they entered the whirlpool in spacetime thus created, or "loop" as he refers to it.

The time traveler could then end up by watching his or herself enter the loop under such circumstances. Nevertheless, as with the wormhole and black hole, one can't go back in time before the creation of "time machine." Accordingly, there are limitations to this method, as well, and that's if it does prove to work. For example, one couldn't go back in time to the Great Chicago Fire, because this would be before the building of the time machine.

**6. Neutrinos Travel Faster Than Light?** Twice now, with the first being in 2011, experiments have shown that the almost massless subatomic particles known as neutrinos seem to be capable of traveling somewhat faster than the speed of light. This, of course, would put the whole idea of the speed of light being an impassable speed limit on very shaky ground, if this is truly so.

With the first result in 2011, so much controversy resulted, with so many detractors claiming flaws in the experiment that most physicists generally discounted the tests as being true. However and much more recently, they repeated the experiment with the flaws fixed this time. The results are still similar. Neutrinos do seem to be able to travel marginally faster than the speed of light if these conclusions hold up. Again, controversy rages. One doesn't mess with Einstein's theories without this happening, it seems.

Nevertheless, if they repeat the experiment with the same outcome, then the speed of light is not the barrier we might think it would be. According to Einstein himself, if something can go faster than the speed of light, it can travel back through time. So of course, the question arises if neutrinos can do this. The final answer remains unclear for now and the truth waits until the researchers finish yet further experiments.

**7. Universe Expanding Faster Than Light?** There seems to be good and considerable evidence that shows this is exactly what is happening. The universe expands, but the rate of expansion has recently been determined to be speeding up! It is not a constant expansion rate, or even slowing down as once thought.

This means that space between the galaxies (and stars, planets, and whatever) is expanding at an ever more rapid rate. Eventually, if it hasn't already happened at the farthest reaches of our universe, and some scientists think it may have, the universe will reach a point where it is expanding so rapidly, it will be expanding faster than the speed of light. This is spacetime itself that is expanding at such a rate, so everything embedded in it, is carried right along with it at such a speed, including even galaxies. Nor does it violate Einstein's theories, because spacetime is expanding this quickly and not the objects embedded in it.

What does this mean? Well, light leaving a far galaxy or galaxies and heading toward us would never make it here with such a speed of expansion as that of faster than light. Nor would light from our galaxy ever reach there, either. Light traveling across the intervening space would never catch up with the receding targets, but instead, be forever chasing and forever falling farther behind.

Again, this violates no laws of physics. This is because spacetime itself is doing the expanding, and not the objects embedded in it that are traveling faster than light. A hard concept for one to wrap one's head around, for sure, but this is just what cosmologists/physicists think might be happening, or will sometime happen in the future of the universe.

What are the implications for time travel? Well, nobody is sure with regard to this one. Still, it makes one wonder what would happen. What if there is a wormhole in our sector of space and the wormhole connects to one in another sector so far away that it is traveling faster than light away from us due to the speed of expanding spacetime? What would be the result for someone traveling through the wormholes? Would we be going back in time or to the future? Again, the answer is unknown. One thing is sure; we would not end up in the same "present." That's a given.

**Conclusion:** These are the main concepts for time travel as we currently understand the scientific possibilities for them right now and based on the *known* laws of physics. I stress the word *"known"* here, because as history has shown us repeatedly, our understanding of physics keeps changing, keeps including more information, and keeps growing and increasing to include more concepts, and some strange ones at that.

As for time travel, please remember that one method is real already, if only to a tiny extent. This has resulted in our Global Positioning System (GPS), needing to constantly be corrected for this time disparity of our satellites in space traveling faster than we are here on Earth, and so slowing down in time accordingly (from our perspective here on Earth).

So is time travel possible? Yes. It would definitely seem so. Moreover, we've done it, at least a tiny bit and using Einstein's Special Theory of Relativity. Still, this is only with regard to traveling into the future. Traveling into the past seems a much harder thing to do.

Nonetheless, as we've seen, there are even ways to travel into the past, apparently. We will look at some other theories of how we could time travel, based on what we know now about the universe and just a little later on in this book.

However, for now, let's move on and concentrate on actual evidence that time travel has already occurred in other ways, and besides just objects moving slightly slower in time because of their speed.

Has time travel already happened? Again, the short answer would appear to be that yes, it has. Do we also have evidence of time travelers? Once more, the answer would be yes, we do. Let's look at some of that evidence in the next chapter.

# CHAPTER 3

# Case Histories Of Time Travel Evidence

*"With a bit of mind flip, you're into a time slip, and nothing...can ever be the same."*

—**Lyrics from** *The Time Warp,*
*The Rocky Horror Picture Show*

Many people have described strange incidences of time travel events occurring. We haven't room for all of them here in this book, obviously, since there are hundreds, even thousands of such testimonies, but we have selected a few of the most outstanding ones, and ones that cover several centuries to show just how long this has been going on. The reason we selected these, some of them very old ones, is to show this sort of thing is not new, not just recent, but has been a sustained phenomenon for a long period in our history.

In addition, yes, whenever reading or listening to such eyewitness accounts of something, a certain amount of skepticism is justified and even necessary, of course. One should have an open mind, but one should also be objective. Therefore, in this book, only those cases where multiple witnesses are involved, or there is other corroborating evidence, are used. This is in order to act as further support for the idea the events actually took place, and that they did happen the way the witnesses described.

One witness may or may not be reliable. Even several can be wrong, but more often this is not the case if there is more than one witness present. People are convicted all the time in court because of the testimony of several witnesses, so since such multiple testimonies do lend credence in the eyes of the law to something being true, this book utilizes the same premise, as well.

**Woman With Cellphone In 1928 Charlie Chaplain Movie?**
[In this movie, a woman seems to be talking into a cellphone long before there were such things. Debunkers say it "might" be a form of hearing aid that was available at the time. Yet, she is alone, walking down a busy street, people passing her on both sides and she is talking to someone...Who would that be if not on a cellphone?]
Video Clip available at:
https://www.youtube.com/watch?v=TiIrpEMbQ2M

Is any particular case absolutely true? No, of course not. Nobody can make such a broad claim.

However, if one takes into account the type of people involved, the number of them, and the nature of the event itself, and the number of such similar events occurring, and if enough people attest to such things as being true, then there is a much higher likelihood of their being truth to many time travel cases. Also, remember, this is just one type of evidence. There are others.

Moreover, as with all such things, the more types of evidence one has, the better chance of proving something as true. Therefore, I will show other types of evidence here, as well. So let's begin and we will start at the beginning with the oldest cases first:

**An Unhappy Marie Antoinette.** This book includes this incident because it is one of the oldest stories of time travel and because it is one of the most famous. Eventually, the victims of the event even wrote an entire book on the subject. This case of time travel took place at the turn of the prior century, in 1901, August 10, 1901, to be exact.

Since then, various authors have written much about the topic ever since. Because of the age of the account, this establishes the idea of people traveling through time as not being a new phenomenon. The case is also included here for this reason, as well.

The story: Two women, Eleanor Jourdain and Charlotte Moberly, were visiting Versailles, the palace and grounds there of former kings and queens of France. Versailles is a fantastic place and one of very real excess, no doubt. The very existence of the place may have added to the fuel that caused the fires of the French Revolution, since the palace and grounds were so over the top by comparison to the miserable lot of the common peasants of France. This resulted in an obvious and glaring disparity between those with wealth and power versus those who had none.

In any case, the two women involved were well educated and had traveled much. They were of "good" reputation, as the term of those days went, and of a good, solid background. The two grown up in "no-nonsense" environments. Neither had they ever shown any inclination to flights of fancy of any sort. There is no record of them ever having shown any overt interest in the supernatural or paranormal, as well.

They also had a strong liking for culture. The arts and history were favorite subjects of theirs. Because of this, they naturally gravitated to visiting such places as Versailles, where so much of it was available. It was while visiting there that the time travel event occurred.

The two women were wandering about the grounds of Versailles when they decided to head for the Petit Trianon, a small chateau constructed by Louis XV over a six-year period, between 1762 and 1768. He had the place built for his then mistress, the famous Madame de Pompadour. Subsequently, it became a place of private refuge for his next mistress, Madame du Barry. Finally, when Louis XVI came to the throne, he turned the place over to his new wife, Queen Marie Antoinette, and again it became a place of special asylum once more, this time for her. It is here our story begins.

Marie Antoinette would retire herself to the chateau, the Petit Trianon, as a place where she could escape the rigors of the court. This was her "fortress of solitude," a bastion against the constant critical eyes and judgmental looks of the courtiers, nobles, and diplomats.

So important was the chateau to her in this regard that everything there was strictly under her control and her control alone. Everything was *de par la Reine,* which in English translates "by order of the Queen." Nobody came or went without her say, not even the king. This love of her privacy I stress here for several reasons:

First, it shows the importance of the place as being Marie Antoinette's own place and nobody else's. Secondly, it shows her strong desire for privacy in the form of such a retreat, even within the extensive palace grounds of Versailles, itself. Thirdly, it gave her ultimate control, but this was at a cost.

Since only certain people had admittance there, such as the Princess de Lamballe among others, those left out of this elite group, the other nobles became not only jealous, but also disaffected from Marie Antoinette. In short, the queen's love of the Petit Trianon only added to the growing number of her enemies at court and they were numerous already.

Marie Antoinette didn't seem to care. She loved the chateau. Nevertheless, her indifference to making enemies eventually helped cost her life, for during the French Revolution that was soon to follow, the royal family was imprisoned and the revolutionaries beheaded the king and queen. Their son, the heir apparent to the throne, the *"Dauphin,"* disappeared entirely. Historians generally believe the revolutionaries murdered him and then disposed of his body.

I include these events here, because some claim the incredibly tragic nature of them allowed the following event to take place. These people argue that such strong emotional happenings can tear fabrics in time, or perhaps "impress" on a place a historical event or scene for others to view much later.

Just about a hundred years later, Charlotte Anne Moberly and her companion, Eleanor Jourdain tried to find the Petit Trianon. However, they soon became disoriented and lost. This sort of thing is common for first-time tourists at such a sprawling place as the grounds of Versailles, but more was to happen to them than just losing their way.

At one point in their quest, a bleak feeling came over them both, as of some type of deep *"oppression and dreariness."* Bewildered as to their true whereabouts, they came across a farmhouse. Here, they saw a woman who waved a "white cloth" out of a window, and it was here, as well, that the feeling of bleakness and loss noticeably increased for them.

Moving on, the women noticed several men, whom they described as "very dignified." They were dressed in long coats, a dull green in color and they all wore tri-cornered hats. The two women simply assumed the men were in period costume dress, for the clothing was of the type worn over a hundred years earlier. They also assumed this was for some sort of pageant, perhaps a typical display for tourists to the area.

This assumption seemed to be confirmed when they later wandered by a cottage. In the entrance stood a woman and girl, also in period dress, and the woman was proffering a jug to the younger woman. MS Jourdain said it looked exactly as if it were a "tableau vivant," as if creating a living picture. This was when the feeling of "oppression" became very strong, and although MS Moberly said she did not notice the cottage, she did feel the onset of the strange feeling along with MS Jourdain. As she later said in a book, the two women wrote:

*"Everything suddenly looked unnatural, therefore unpleasant; even the trees seemed to become flat and lifeless, like wood worked in tapestry. There were no effects of light and shade, and no wind stirred the trees."*

Farther on, they saw a man sitting near a gazebo, or garden kiosk. He wore a long dark cloak and a wide-brimmed hat shadowed his face. MS Moberly later referred to his facial appearance as being *"most repulsive,"* and *"its expression odious."* He appeared to have suffered severely in the past from smallpox. She also said that:

*"The man slowly turned his face, which was marked by smallpox; his complexion was very dark. The expression was evil and yet unseeing, and though I did not feel that he was looking particularly at us, I felt a repugnance to going past him."*

A littler farther on, a man with a "sombrero" like hat, directed them on toward the Petit Trianon. MS Moberly, later on, in their wandering to find the chateau, noticed a woman sketching, and according to her, the woman bore a striking resemblance to Queen Marie Antoinette, as she had appeared in a painting by the artist, Wertmüller. MS Moberly described the woman as being dressed simply in a summer dress, and wearing a hat.

At first, MS Moberly mistook her for another tourist, but then realized that she, too, was dressed in what seemed to be period costuming. Later, MS Moberly felt she had seen Marie Antoinette. MS Jourdain did not see her. Why this was is so is uncertain, but both women seemed to have noticed things the other did not, as if some things were visible to one, but not the other.

After this, the two women seemed to have returned to their own time. They found their way back to their accommodations. At first, neither talked about the incident, but after a week or so, they finally did, if reluctantly, because the episode had upset both of them. Later, home again, they eventually wrote a book, but by no means immediately. In fact, it was years later.

The book became popular for the time. Some people believed the two women, while others felt the whole thing was some sort of hoax. Since that first book, many others have included the episode in their own works, and the incident has been the subject of discussions for over a hundred years now.

Was the episode a hoax? Well, it could have been, but there are factors that weigh against this idea. Again, the two women were extremely well educated. They were of "good families," ones known for being practical, down-to-earth, and solid middle class.

Moreover, they had never shown any inclination of any sort to perpetrate hoaxes or for that matter any types of flights of fancy, either.

Furthermore, in those days they had much to lose, such as their status in society, their personal reputations for being "educated," and their standings for truthfulness, as well, among other things. At the beginning of the last century, once such things were lost, they were virtually irretrievable in the rigid discipline of the society of the day.

In addition, they felt they had little to obtain in the way of personal gain by writing the book, because such books usually only sold to fringe elements and so didn't make much money. Therefore, they did not have any real expectations in this regard, that of gaining wealth, although as it turns out, the book did ultimately sell fairly well.

There is another factor here to be considered; if people were planning to perpetrate a hoax in order to gain notoriety, if of a not very favorable sort or notoriety, why wait so very long, until 1911, to write the book, *An Adventure*? Moreover, if they sought fame, why use pseudonyms instead of their own names? People who commit hoaxes usually do so to gain attention and/or money. Furthermore, they don't usually wait an entire decade to do this. They certainly don't in today's world!

The two women again visited Versailles, and repeatedly, but were never able to find the route they had taken the first time and despite their best efforts. If they were committing a hoax, then why not claim once again that they had stumbled on things they had seen before, or other scenes of a similar nature? After all, they could well then have written yet another book.

They did not. The path they had taken, like the rest of it, had vanished and they had only seen it the once. They made no claims to ever having found it again, despite those repeated visits and in part making those trips for just that purpose.

In conclusion, it seems likely the two women did witness something truly unusual. Controversy still goes on as to whether this was a ghostly visitation or a form of time travel. Adherents of the ghost theory used the fact of the feeling of "oppression and dreariness." They said this was clearly an emotional overtone of some importance, and supported the idea of this being a supernatural and otherworldly event. However, the clarity of what the two women had seen, the fact one woman saw some things while the other saw different things, tends to tilt the argument in the favor of the time travel theory.

This might have been a "repeater" ghost experience. These are where some event from the past seems to play out repeatedly. However, even ghost hunters acknowledge these are probably not actual ghost sightings, but rather some event in history somehow managing to play itself out repeatedly in later times, having been "impressed" on the area or local region for some reason, either through electromagnetic or psychic means. The exact cause of this phenomenon is also a cause for much conjecture.

Yet, there are problems even with this idea. The women actually interacted with some of the people from the past, and so did not just witness events, as if unfolding on some stage before them. They spoke to people. They communicated with them in a very ordinary sort of way.

This lends credence to the idea they actually had passed back in time, but it must have been a halting sort of time travel, half-real, and half-unformed, with one woman witnessing some things, while the other witnessed others. One might say there was sort of an overlay of the present with the past going on there, and it wasn't a complete overlay, but only a partial one.

Still, they did see things in common, as well, and although one may talk to a ghost, it doesn't usually answer back in coherent sentences and/or give mundane directions to those who are lost and seek such help, as happened with the two women. Such would be very accommodating ghosts, indeed, if this were so. Therefore, the idea they were just witnessing something doesn't describe their experiences accurately. They were *involved* in the event, as well.

**Summary of Event:** It would seem the women, MS Moberly and MS Jourdain, witnessed something from the real past. The fact the event had strong emotional overtones might well have been the feeling one might get when passing through to another time, a sort of side effect of a temporal (time) translocation of such a sort. Furthermore, the "flatness" they saw and felt, along with the lack of shadows, might have been a part of this temporal passage experience. When one moves from one reality to another, one time to another and back, there could well be strange side effects in doing so, and these could include psychological ones easily enough.

In any case, this is one of the earliest and most well documented cases of people witnessing and even interacting with events from another time. Whether this was true time travel or some sort of massive ghostly manifestation, which would seem to have amounted to pretty much the same thing for all practical purposes, is less certain.

However, the two women think it was a form of time travel or trans-temporal location, and given the evidence, it would seem to fit this idea far better than that of being some sort of ghostly experience.

Furthermore, since the people met and spoke with didn't act in any way like tortured souls or trapped ghosts, and even answered their questions in a normal manner, it would appear the idea of this having been a form of time travel would seem to be the most likely conclusion. (For links to this incident, please see *"References"* at the end of this book.)

**The Paralyzed Woman.** This incident comes to us from South America. More exactly, it is from Lima, Peru. A doctor, Raul Rios Centeno, swears this event actually took place. He first became aware of the whole thing when a young woman had an appointment with him. As it turned out, just half of her body seemed paralyzed with what was, he thought at first, all the typical symptoms of a condition known as hemiplegia. This literally means the same thing, someone who suffers from having one-half of their body paralyzed. Trying to determine the cause, he inquired after when and how the symptoms had first come upon her.

The woman stated she had been vacationing near the Stone Forest of Markahuasi when the paralysis took place. She told the doctor of how, one night, she had been exploring, even if a little late for her to do this. She was with friends at the time.

It was then they heard music in the distance, and following the sound, came upon a small stone cottage. The place seemed to have no electricity, because burning torches were the only apparent source of light coming from the place.

By their glow, through the windows and doorway, they glimpsed people dancing. However, the participants were dressed in a decidedly out-of-date way. They wore 1600's-style clothing.

Intrigued, and just assuming the people were simply having a costume party or special festival of some sort, they moved toward the cottage. The young woman advanced to the open door and started to step inside. However, as she approached the place, she said she felt a sudden chill, a penetrating coldness, but she thought little about this, being still too intrigued to see what was going on in the cabin. Even as she tried to go inside, one of her friends, another woman tugged on her arm and pulled her back out. The young woman immediately felt a numbness penetrate one side of her body. It was at the exact moment she had withdrawn from the doorway that the hemiplegia or half-paralysis symptoms overcame her.

Later, after performing tests on her, the doctor concluded that the left side of her brain did not seem to be functioning normally, having an *"abnormal amount of electric waves,"* as one article put it. The doctor is even now at a loss as to explain how this could be, or if the condition will ever clear itself, for he had nothing he could prescribe as a treatment for her condition.

The question arises if the young woman had stepped through time, or started to, in trying to enter a cottage full of people who may have been from another point in history. The half of her that had started to enter might have been affected by passing between two different times, her present time, and the costumed people's past time, and then being jerked back again. The sudden and intense feeling of cold might have been a symptom of this happening to her.

**Summary of Event.** One thing is certain; the woman had no reason to lie about her condition. Additionally, the paralysis is real and verifiable. Nevertheless, the cause of her condition is completely unknown. The fact there were also several witnesses to the event also lends a good deal of credence to this account.

What does this all mean? What really happened? Well, it is a fact that a young woman, along with others, saw a primitive stone cabin full of people dressed as if from another time. Upon trying to enter the place, and only pulled back out at the last minute, the same young woman ended up by being half-paralyzed, and it was the half of her body that had started to enter the cabin. Something very strange happened at that moment, and for many, it is an example of time travel. More importantly, it's an example of what can happen when time travel goes wrong. For more information on this, please see the link under "*References*" at the end of this book.

**The "Time Slip" Flight.** This case keeps popping up repeatedly, and with good reason; the credentials of the person involved were excellent! None could be better. A Royal Air Force Senior Commander, Robert Goddard (later to become Sir Robert Goddard), told of a very strange event. In fact, so odd was this incident for him that it colored his opinions of things to the point where he later became very interested in the whole subject of UFOs. Perhaps the best retelling of this incident is in J.H. Brennan's *Time Travel: A New Perspective*. For reasons of space, here is a necessarily much briefer version of the event, but includes the main facts.

Sir Robert Goddard was a pilot for the Royal Air Force and his record as a pilot was a very good one, outstanding, in fact. Having fought in both world wars, he was also a highly educated man, as well, with an engineering degree from Cambridge University.

The event in question took place not long before the outbreak of World War II, which for England was in 1939. The year at the time was 1935. Sir Robert had just accepted the lofty position of Deputy Director of Intelligence for the British Air Ministry. I mention Sir Robert's background here to stress his reliability as a witness, and as far as such backgrounds go, this one would be hard to beat.

Sir Robert had flown from Andover to Edinburgh, Scotland. He flew over Drem where he saw an abandoned and rundown airfield, one long in disuse, judging by the crumbing state of the buildings and the tarmac. This was not out of the ordinary in and of itself, until, just days later, on his return trip, he again flew over the same area.

This time, the flight encountered strange stormy weather and Sir Robert later remarked on how yellow the clouds looked, how odd, and it was a sight he had never seen before. Sir Robert became confused, bewildered, because of the storm. As a result, he began to lose control over his plane. His aircraft started descending after first having climbed. Goddard's intent was to clear the cloud layer somehow and so regain his sense of orientation.

Having once finally cleared the yellowish clouds, he saw below him the Drem airbase once more. At this point, and quite suddenly, the storm and clouds that had caused his disorientation abruptly dissipated, as if the tempest had never been.

However, this time when he looked at the airfield, the place appeared occupied and in good repair. Gone were the cracks and the heaving tarmac with the plants that had forced their way through fissures there. Instead, there were four planes sitting on the landing field. They were yellow in color and one of them was of an unfamiliar type to him. Moreover, there were what appeared to be mechanics there, as well, but they were wearing unfamiliar blue outfits.

Having regained control of his plane completely now, Sir Robert Victor Goddard continued on his journey without attempting to land at the airfield. He arrived at his destination without further incident and everything was as it should be. However, he was naturally bewildered by what he had seen, so much so, that he chose not to speak of it to anyone, for fear of repercussions in the form of ridicule or disbelief. He also feared some might even go so far as to doubt his sanity. This was an understandable fear under the circumstances. He had a brilliant career he did not wish to jeopardize by speaking up.

Within four years, the Royal Air Force began painting some of their planes yellow. Furthermore, they began switching to monoplanes instead of biplanes, one of the exact type he'd seen parked on the runway at Drem on his journey home. Moreover, the RAF also had its mechanics adopt the same blue color uniforms as Goddard had seen the men wearing at Drem. The British had repaired the airfield and again placed it into service. Subsequently, for the duration of World War II, the place was an active base.

**Summary of Event.** Sir Robert Victor Goddard became convinced he had traveled forward in time, and had witnessed the airbase, as it would appear a number of years in the future. One wonders what he would have done if he had landed at the airfield instead of flying on. Would he trapped himself in that future time? Alternatively, was what he saw just a glimpse of things to come, just a look or quick vision into the future?

No one will ever know the answers to these questions now, it seems. However, Sir Robert Goddard was firmly convinced that what he had seen was real. Again, this so affected his thinking about such things that after the war, he became highly interested in the subject of UFOs. He was looking for answers as to what had happened to him in 1935, and he would continue to look for them for the rest of his life.

**The Flight Through Time Of Bruce Gernon.** This incident is included despite many people already having heard of it, and out of chronological order, because it has many similarities to Sir Robert Victor Goddard's event. Therefore, I felt it best to place the two events together here. The pilot in this case was Bruce Gernon and his flight included his father as a passenger. Bruce had been a pilot for some time and had flown in part of the area now known as the Bermuda Triangle many times before, so he was familiar with the conditions there. Furthermore, he had never before experienced anything weird or out of the ordinary in any of his flights.

However, on one flight in December of 1970, as the journey progressed, he noticed an "elliptical" shaped cloud ahead of him. He tried to climb above it, but even as he approached the cloud, it rapidly grew in height. Despite his best efforts to fly over the cloud, his plane was enveloped. Bruce said he was plunged into an almost complete darkness. This occurred just off Andros Island and the cloud was big! At this point, Mr. Gernon described the cloud as "doughnut-shaped," and according to Bruce, he traveled on through it for some thirteen miles before he saw what appeared to be an opening.

Feeling he had no choice but to take the opportunity, Mr. Gernon headed for the opening, a "u-shaped" one, as he described it. As he approached, the tops of the clouds above the opening came together, now forming a tunnel of sorts through which he flew. There was blue sky showing on the other end of the "tunnel," so Bruce continued his flight in that direction, hoping to win free of the cloud at last.

However, as he and his father flew on through the tunnel, the thing took on a spiral shape and started to contract as they made their way. Bruce knew it would be a close thing between making it to the blue sky beyond and once again swallowed in the vortex-like tunnel of impenetrable cloud as it closed in about their plane.

He had some distance yet to travel because the tunnel, approximately a mile wide, was about ten miles long at the time, according to Bruce. However, by the time he had entered the tunnel, it had already shrunk to just about 200 feet across. The only good news was now the thing seemed only about a mile in length, instead of the original ten miles he had estimated. Mr. Gernon cannot account for these rapid changes in size of the tunnel and the distance to traverse it, but merely notes them as a factor in his progress.

Not long later, they emerged from the tunnel, which as Mr. Gernon looked back, closed to a mere slit of rotating cloud behind them, looking very much, apparently, like a whirlpool that had formed inside of the cloud itself. At this point, all the electronic gear on the plane ceased to function, or to function in any normal manner. Mr. Gernon later referred to this anomaly as an "electronic fog."

Bruce flew the plane on by feel alone, since his instruments no longer functioned correctly. Three minutes passed before the instrumentation returned to normal, as if nothing had ever been wrong with them. When contacted a few moments later, a ground control operator identified them as now being over Miami.

There total flight time to this point had been a mere thirty-four minutes. By the time he landed the plane, the total flight time had been some forty-seven minutes on a trip that at a minimum, should have taken seventy-five.

As Bruce put it, they had traveled about one hundred miles in approximately three minutes. Bruce Gernon was convinced that traveling through the cloud "vortex" had somehow pushed them forward through time and space. Mr. Gernon is adamant to this day that he went through this weird event, and just as he and his father both claim it occurred.

**Conclusion:** The two above incidents of moving forward in time while on flights do have very similar aspects to them. Both involved flights of small planes that encountered odd clouds and/or storms. Both related that their planes apparently then jumped forward in time.

For Bruce Gernon, the jump was a permanent one, but for Sir Robert Victor Goddard, it was not, but more of just a visit before returning to his own time. The major differences are in the descriptions of the clouds, although both described them as being out of the ordinary and unusual, and in how far they jumped in time, one about half an hour or so, while the other at least four years before returning to his own time.

Why this major difference? Well, one reason might be that Sir Robert Victor Goddard didn't land at the airfield of the future he saw, but continued his flight, while Bruce did land his plane in Miami. Although, in Bruce's case, it appeared he had little choice. He, unlike Sir Robert seemed to make a time transition that did not allow for going back again.

Perhaps, Sir Robert, as mentioned above, had just "seen" the future airfield, as if through some sort of time telescope effect, but had not actually gone through time to the future. He, unlike Bruce Gernon, had not gone through a vortex, so he may simply have seen the future from afar, so to speak, a vision of what was to come before passing on by the time "lens" that was showing this to him.

In any case, judging by these events, one can assume that forward travel through time/space does seem to be possible, "if" one takes these accounts as true. Since both seem to be from reliable sources, at the very least, something very strange concerning time happened to all those involved.

**Photo of Sir Robert Victor Goddard**

Again, let's remember there are more such accounts of these sorts of trips through time, and that these are hardly the only ones. Therefore, we are not relying solely on these for evidence as just singular and unusual tales of such happenings, but also by the number of such tales overall, as well. Again, there are many more. Please see *"References"* at the end of this book for links to more such accounts.

Are these tales true? Well, again, as with the Versailles story, the people involved had little reason to create hoaxes. In fact, in the case of Sir Robert Victor Goddard, such a tale could only damage an otherwise pristine and impressive reputation he had acquired by that time.

For Mr. Gernon and his father to falsify such a thing seems to be equally pointless. They had little to gain and much to lose. Ridicule of those claiming such things is the given. Moreover, neither one publicly came out with the story at the time of the occurrence, so immediate notoriety was not their aim, it seems, any more than it was for the two women who went to Versailles.

Still, people do commit hoaxes, of course. This, we have to definitely consider. Yet, in these particular instances, it is hard to see how or why the people involved would do such a thing. Why not try to take immediate advantage of it in either the form of notoriety and fame, and/or making money. In both cases, as with the two women at Versailles, as well, nobody said anything at the time, nor for a long time after. Years passed in some cases, before anyone spoke of the events.

In the next chapter, we'll look at some other apparent time travel instances, as well. One final thing to note here, though, is that these incidents took place decades apart, one before World War II, and the other in the latter half of the $20^{th}$ Century. Therefore, it is clear there is a pattern of sorts established here, what with the two women of Versailles being involved, and evens others before them. Time travel, it seems, doesn't just occur in any single time, but throughout history, as well.

# CHAPTER 4
# More Cases Of Time Travel

*"[A] scientific basis for time travel was established more than a hundred years ago… Albert Einstein and Hermann Minkowski showed how it was theoretically possible in 1905 and 1908."*

**—Wolf, Fred Alan, The Yoga of Time Travel**

Time travel incidents don't seem to be just limited to those who fly in small planes, or even fly at all, as we've seen with the women who visited Versailles. Time shifting events seem to occur right here on the ground, as well. Moreover, public streets seem to be a favorite place for these to occur.

**Liverpool Time Travel Street.** There are several accounts of people who have claimed time travel on, or very near Bold Street in Liverpool, England. Now, taken at first glance, the story of one person walking along the street and then transported through time would not seem to be a very strong piece of evidence. In fact, taken on its own, such a thing isn't much in the way of evidence at all.

After all, a lone person can claim anything. However, in this case, we include Bold Street here, because no less than five different people at five different times claim the same thing happened to them on or very near Bold Street! The people involved also don't seem to be of the type to commit hoaxes, as well, but rather being the sort who are "very down to Earth," and not prone to fanciful ideas. These cases, referenced from *Edge of Time* by author Tim Swartz, but also from other independent sources, as well, including information by Tom Slemen. (See, *"References"*), all seem to have much in common.

Can you pick out the supposed Time Traveler at this 1941 Bridge Opening in Canada?

[If you picked the man in the sunglasses, you picked the one people are talking about. Everybody picks him. Detractors say that the glasses, the shirt with the "M" on it, even the camera were possibly available at the time, if very rare items. Yet, here we see them all in one place at one "time" on one man, at a time when the camera, for instance, was exceedingly rare, and so were those sunglasses, etc. So are the debunkers right? Or is he from another time?]

~50~

Moreover, the fact everyone immediately spots him as the possible time travelers says much, as well. Notice he's taller than anyone else there, even the men sitting on the cars in the background? Everyone is shorter than him. And the average height of people has increased markedly since 1941...]

**The First Case, Lunchtime In The Past:** This incident is very reminiscent in some respects of the Versailles account, for it involves interaction with another person, as do many time travel stories. In this case, a woman who was quite the skeptic when it came to anything of a supernatural nature had a strange encounter.

She had a job in the Liverpool city center area. This was in the 1980's. On her lunch breaks, she would sit outdoors on a bench and enjoy her meals there whenever possible. Being England, often the weather did not allow for this, so she took the opportunity whenever it arose and as often as she could.

One day, she chose a bench near Waterstones Book Shop. This was on Bold Street. As she took her place on the bench, an odd thing happened. The sun, which had been bright just moments before and so had been the reason for her deciding to eat her lunch outdoors, suddenly seemed dimmer, less bright or powerful in an odd sort of way.

In retrospect, she would later say it reminded her of a time there had been a partial solar eclipse, for the light had dimmed that much, but much more swiftly in this case. Again, please note here that we have that odd change in lighting, even as the women at Versailles had experienced.

As she began her meal, a man seated next to her struck up a polite conversation. He was well dressed, but the woman, after several cursory and guarded inspections of him, realized his style of dress was well out of date. In fact, he was dressed in the style of clothing of someone from the early 1950's, at the very least.

Another thing that caught her attention was how relatively empty Bold Street seemed of a sudden, and this at lunch hour, when there was usually a throng of people, either getting lunch or running errands before returning to work. Of course, some days, saw more people than others, but this seemed an unusually low turnout by any measure.

She continued her casual conversation with the man as she ate. Then, at one point, she turned slightly from him to throw the packaging from her sandwich into the trashcan next to the bench. She had been responding to a question the man had asked, and continued to do so even as she threw away the wrapper.

The woman claims her eyes were off the man no more than an instant, just long enough to toss the trash into the container next to her. However, when she turned back, the man had vanished. She never laid eyes upon him again. He was nowhere in sight in the open area, either. At the same moment, the sun brightened noticeably and Bold Street's normal throng of lunchtime people appeared to be the normal amount again, with the standard hustle and bustle she had come to expect there.

The woman is at a loss as to explain these events, but she had the unnerving feeling that perhaps she had entered the past for a number of minutes and while having her lunch, no less.

She even spoke to a man she felt was out of time, either that, or she had transferred in time to another and prior decade in which he lived for a few minutes. Either way, it was her certainty that some weird time episode had occurred for her.

**Second Case, A Walk Into History.** A man, who had lived a long time in Liverpool and worked on Bold Street, also had an interesting time travel experience. He took a walk one day, making his way to Bold Street as he did so. Being a longtime resident of Liverpool, he was well aware of the changes that had occurred over time in the area he walked through. This included changes in businesses, the closing of various shops and kiosks over the years, and the opening of new ones, although these were fewer in numbers of these.

One of the businesses that had closed some years before was "Collinsons," along with many others, since the area had slowly been going downhill for some time. However, on this walk, upon arriving on Bold Street, he noticed that Collinsons was in business once more, for there now was a display of items in the window.

At the same time, he also noticed another place; and oddity "Catchpoles" was back in its original location across the street from Collinsons. Catchpoles, a shop, had relocated a few years before to another site. The man thought it was odd that it had chosen then to relocate back to the same place, and even odder that Collinsons, which he had assumed was defunct, should now have reopened at the same time.

There was more. The vehicles moving up and down Bold Street were all a decade or more old. There were no recent ones. Pedestrians also seemed out of date, wearing clothes that although not very strange, or outré, still seemed at least a decade or more behind the current times.

Thinking some special occasion might be taking place, as in some sort of historical or commercial pageant he had not heard of, he did not dwell too long on this aspect of things. However, as with the woman on the bench, he did notice the street was not heavily trafficked, as it usually was, that both cars and pedestrians were in smaller numbers. This, too, seemed odd, since if this was a historical pageant, there should have been a more than usual crowd drawn to the area, but not less.

Meeting up with his wife outside of a bank on another street, he and his spouse then went inside the building. Everything seemed fine there. No one was oddly dressed or wearing clothes that appeared out of date. When they left the building and walked back the way he had come, the man noticed everything had reverted to the way he had become accustomed to seeing it over the last few years. Gone were almost all the old cars, except for a few worn looking ones. There were more pedestrians and traffic, as well. The shoppers' clothes seemed up to date now, and the Collinsons' had disappeared. Moreover, Catchpoles had shifted back again to its more modern location. Furthermore, shops that had again held businesses on his last walk were now empty and closed again.

The man was nonplussed. He felt sure he had walked down Bold Street and somehow had done so when it was ten to fifteen years in his past. His wife, who had not made the original trip with him, was unaware of any unusual changes at all.

Furthermore, the man couldn't be certain when the street changed back to the present. He didn't know, whether it was before he entered the bank, or after, but changed back, it had at some point.

**Third Case, Man Sees Dead Grandmother At Train Station.** A man at the Liverpool Central train station was making his way down a stairway one day, heading for the platform his train was due to arrive at. Liverpool Central had undergone major modifications over the prior few years, as so many stations had during this period. This was in order to update them to accommodate more passengers and generally to modernize everything. Therefore, things had changed as to where staircases and walkways were located. Engineers had rerouted or shifted many of them.

Prior to these changes, debarking passengers from trains were required to climb a long staircase to exit the platform. At the top of the stairs in those days, one had to turn left to exit onto the adjacent street.

The man was on a set of stairs on the opposite side of the tracks from where the old and longer staircase had once been when he noticed an old woman on the other side, seemingly climbing the old staircase. Startled, he realized it was his grandmother leaving the station, for there was no doubt as to this. He had a clear view of her.

Moreover, she, like the fictional Miss Marple of Agatha Christie's murder mysteries, had always worn out-of-date clothes, even for the times she lived in. These were of the 1930's style. This woman was wearing such clothes now, and they were wildly anachronistic for the current times.

The man double-checked the woman to be certain. Again, he had no doubt this was his grandmother leaving the station. However, there was a major problem; his grandmother had been dead for some years by this point! Even so, there she was. The man took off back up the stairs, fighting the descending masses of people, who blocked his way and slowed him down.

He struggled to get to her. At one point, glancing over at his grandmother, he saw her make a left turn after having finished climbing the flight of stairs.

Now, she headed to the street. He followed her just seconds later, but upon making the same turn, found she was gone. His grandmother had vanished, had utterly disappeared. The old long staircase was no longer in sight, either.

The man is insistent upon a number of points about all of this: (1) He was sure it was his grandmother and not a look-alike. (2) He can't account for her having been there, since she had been long dead. (3) The man felt sure she couldn't have dashed off before he caught up to her. His grandmother was an old woman, frail, and quite incapable of making such an enormous effort as to deliberately try to escape him. She was, after all, well into her 70's before she died. Moreover, why would she had done such a thing, tried to avoid him?

The man couldn't explain how or why this happened to him. He had long since gotten over her death, so he wasn't suffering any sort of severe grief when the event occurred. For this reason, he feels what he experienced was not a hallucination, one brought on by strong emotions. He feels he really did see his grandmother, or so he insisted, and she was climbing a staircase from another time. He is adamant about this aspect of the whole affair.

By the way, the street his grandmother would have exited onto would have been Casey Street, which is close by Bold Street. This next case also concerns that same street.

**Fourth Case, A Church Of Another Time.** In this instance, a man who had been on Bold Street decided to go by way of Casey Street to meet up with a companion. As he passed the church at the top of Casey Street, he noticed lights coming from inside the building.

This was strange, because St. Luke had been bombed during World War II. To date, no one had started repairs on the place. Even the roof was, for all practical purposes, nonexistent. The place was not in useable condition as a result and was little more than a ruin. So how and why would there be lights inside of it, as if a service was in progress?

The man was incredulous to learn that not only the church had been renovated and so quickly, but without his having heard of it happening at all. Certainly, such a feat would have been big local news. Still and despite his surprise, he continued on his way. He had a friend to meet and didn't want to be late.

However, later on, while again passing the church, this time near close to the Christmas holidays, to his complete bewilderment, he saw the church was again plunged into darkness and in a dismal state of disrepair. He couldn't account for this, except to think that on the first occasion, he had witnessed the place as it was before the German blitz of Liverpool during the war.

He felt certain that somehow, he had caught a glimpse of how it had once been in the past. This meant that one night he somehow had either passed through time, or been able at least to see how the church looked on another night long ago and before the devastating Second World War.

**Conclusion:** Here we have no less than five incidents that have taken place around one particular area of the City of Liverpool and all have to do with people somehow viewing or stepping into the past for good amounts of time. No vortices were involved or weird weather, other than in one case, where the woman on the bench noticed a dimming of the sun, as if an eclipse was suddenly occurring.

The remarkable thing about all these events is how consistent they are in their details. People are few in numbers, as they would be in the past, since the population of the city was smaller then. The clothing was out of phase with the present, looking antiquated or anachronistic.

In addition, shops, long closed were not only open again, but in their original locations. Various other buildings, as well, also appeared in their earlier states. Even a church appeared as it had before having been bombed into ruins.

This consistency is a remarkable factor, for it tells us whatever was happening to these people, was happening in pretty much the same way. Moreover, it was always the past that appeared to these people in an around Bold Street, not the future, as it with the prior to flying, time-travel events.

What is there about the area that people can drift in and out of the past? What specifically with regard to Bold Street allows time to come unstuck, as it were, and permit travel to another time?

Just how long this may have been going on for in that area is uncertain, but it would be interesting to determine just how long the Bold Street Phenomenon might have really been going on. Is it just a postwar phenomenon of Liverpool, or is something that has existed for far longer?

We may never know why Bold Street and its immediate environs is subject to such temporal disruptions, how it is people can travel to the past and back in so gentle a manner there, but it is still intriguing to know that something like this exists.

It seems that sometimes, time travel doesn't involve storms, whirlpools in the clouds, or much of anything. It's almost as if in some locations on Earth, one can more or less just slip into another time without even being aware of it happening at first. As we shall see later on this book, people not only seem to slip into other times, but they may well be slipping into alternate timelines or realities, as well…

# CHAPTER 5

# Yet More Cases Of Time Travel

*"Originally, the burden of proof was on physicists to prove that time travel was possible. Now the burden of proof is on physicists to prove there must be a law forbidding time travel."*

— Michio Kaku

Bold Street and Casey Street are not the only places in the Liverpool area to have this weird sort of time incursion. Nearby areas, as well, also have experienced such curious phenomena, as with the village of Thingwall.

**The Thingwall Incident.** This is the story of a young woman who moved to the town of Thingwall. The town is less than eight miles away and across the Mersey River from Liverpool with its infamous, time-distorting Bold Street. This lends credence to the idea that perhaps certain locations are more prone to allowing people to slip through time than others, as if they were areas that were weak spots in the fabric of spacetime in some way. In any case, although not on Bold Street, this event took place not so very far away from it.

Furthermore, it has all the hallmarks of a Bold Street type of event in its details.

Not long after moving to Thingwall, a young mother took her little daughter for an outing, pushing the little girl along ahead of her in a stroller. The woman then decided to take a route through an area of the town she was still unfamiliar with, having only lived in the village a short time at this point. She wished to explore more of the place.

She made her way down a small lane, Mill Lane. The first thing she noticed was that after only walking the lane a short distance, the smooth surface of the road gave way to a more ancient cobblestoned one. This didn't surprise her. Such things in England were hardly a rarity.

After a bit, she passed by a small cottage. There, to her right was an older man smoking a pipe as he leaned against the fence. Out of politeness, she nodded to him, and he returned the gesture, but they did not speak, seeming content to remain quiet and contemplative, rather than to converse with her. This didn't surprise her.

Moving along with her daughter, the woman passed a series of such cottages, all in good repair, and complete with their colorful displays of seasonal flowers growing about them in the front and side gardens. These were on her left. On her right was what seemed a circular commons area, and it, too, had flowers growing there. Beyond the commons was a row of cottages very similar to the others, but with one difference; there was also an arched entryway to a stables area, one made of brick.

Moving still further along, the woman passed a lady dressed in an old style, complete with long dark skirt, a high-collared top, and with a shawl wrapped around her shoulders for warmth, although the day wasn't a cold one. However, they did not speak, as the lady was entering her house just as the woman with her daughter passed by.

Where the lane petered out finally was a gate barring further travel. Atop the gate was a young girl seated there, who, as the woman later described it, was dressed as if she were a character from the television show, Little House On The Prairie. Her dress was of the same style and even her shoes were of the same period, being old-fashioned, buttoned ones.

The woman thought this was decidedly strange, but the girl didn't linger, so she had no chance to speak to her. Instead, the child jumped down from the gate and ran into the cottage nearby, disappearing from sight.

At this point, the woman felt she dared go no further, because beyond the fence was an open green meadow, which was not the best type of terrain to try to push a stroller on. Therefore, she turned around and headed back the way she had come, once again nodding to the old man who still lounged in his front garden there as she passed by. Again, he nodded back and she continued on her way.

After finishing her walk, the young woman related her trip to her mother who later visited her, describing how quaint the lane was, and how antiquated the inhabitants of it seemed to be, as if being from another time.

After this, life as it has a habit of doing, intruded and it wasn't until several more months had passed before she was able to go with her mother down the lane again. She wanted to show the older woman the charming area, as she felt it to be, what with all the baskets of flowers and flowerbeds and all and quaint homes lining the lane there.

Things had changed and the changes weren't all for the better. The smooth paving of the lane now continued. There were no more cobblestones to be seen anywhere.

The picturesque and well cared for cottage where the old man had smoked his pipe was now rundown, boarded up, and decidedly neglected looking, being nothing short of derelict.

Where neat cottages had been nearby with their bright front gardens, there were now a couple of more modern semi-detached houses. The commons area further on, with the once-colorful flowers planted by it, had vanished, as well, along with the brick-arched entryway beyond. They also passed a pile of rubble off to one side on their walk, as they had made their way down the little road. The young woman was sure this heap of stones was the remains of a mill she had seen standing there in good repair on her previous visit.

At the end of the lane, the fence was no more, and neither was the green meadow beyond. Instead, there were a large number of more modern, one-story homes, complete with small front yards and paved road passing in front of them. Where once an open field had stood was now a subdivision.

The young woman was at a loss. These changes were too great, too vast, and made in much too short a time, as far she was concerned. She simply could not account for this massive transformation of the once quaint lane she had traveled to her mother. That it was the same lane, she had no doubt, but it had been altered and dramatically so. What truly through her, was that all this had come about in so inconceivably short a time. In fact, she felt it was impossible.

What had happened to her picturesque and charming lane, and how it had happened so quickly, was a complete mystery to her, but one she didn't actively pursue.

After all, in several months' time, it was at least barely conceivable she supposed that such substantial changes could happen, if however unlikely... Still, there had to be some reasonable explanation for it, she felt.

It wasn't until almost a decade later when the young woman became involved with a right-of-way issue that she discovered something bizarre. To help resolve the problem of the right-of-way, she checked the public references for the area and discovered a map done in 1830. Thingwall Village, as depicted on the map, was much smaller then, of course.

Even so, she found the lane she had walked. Moreover, it was just as it had been when she had walked down Mill Lane. The map depicted the lane as she had first seen it, with the buildings situated just as she had viewed them, the mill, the mews, the commons, the cottages, and the meadow beyond. They were all there.

Therefore, the lane had once existed and just as she had seen it and described it to her mother. The people she had seen there had dressed and looked like they might have in the 19th Century. The layout she had witnessed in person had been exactly as the tithe map had shown it once to be.

How the young woman had managed to walk down a lane and through another time to almost a century earlier was incomprehensible to her, yet she felt she and her daughter had done just this, and even had interacted with the people of that time. She was convinced that somehow, she and her daughter had passed back through time, had walked a lane of another century, only to then have it vanish once more.

**Time Travel Not Just For Those Who Fly.** An article in the 1988 *Strange Magazine (2)* edition by author, Ken Meaux, and titled: *Time Traveler,* shows that time travel isn't just restricted to people flying in planes or walking down streets. Those who drive highways also seem to experience such bizarre events, as well. Here is one of them:

A man, who the author of the article calls "L.C.," was driving down a highway not far from Abbeville, Louisiana. This was October 20, 1969. Along with him was another man, a business associate. They were chatting as they drove northward on Highway 167 toward the city of Lafayette. At this point, they were on a very rural and flat stretch of highway. Traffic was light. It was fall and the time of day was not long after lunch. The weather was clear but cool, so there were no heat waves coming off the highway to cause blurring of vision or any sort of optical illusions.

Along the deserted stretch of highway, they finally noticed a car ahead of them. Gaining on it, they realized the thing was a virtual antique with a "turtle back," as the article refers to the vehicle, which means a sloping rear trunk area. Today, we would refer to it as a "fast back, or perhaps "hatch back."

Intrigued by such an ancient vehicle, they began talking about it, principally admiring the fact that such an old car was still in such marvelous condition. Both men found the pristine state of the thing impressive, the way it still looked so new.

However, the car was a bit of an obstacle, since the thing traveled at a very low rate of speed. L.C.'s business associate, called "Charlie" in the article, decided to go around the old vehicle.

They had appointments to keep and they would be late if they didn't keep moving along at a decent clip. Two-lane highways at the time could be slow enough as it was to travel, without tailing along for endless miles behind an antique vehicle incapable of doing any real speed.

Passing was no problem. There were no oncoming cars to worry about, and the antique was traveling slowly in any case, so they easily and quickly overtook it. For this reason, they didn't hurry in doing this. They wanted to get a better look at a car that was by their time, extremely rare.

They noticed the license plate had "1940" on it in large print. This surprised them, because both knew that using an out-of-date license plate, especially one this way out of date, was undoubtedly breaking the law, even for antique and classic cars. An out-of-date license plate might be allowable specifically for use in parades and such, but not for everyday travel on open highways or public streets.

As they began to draw even, both men took the opportunity to check the car out more thoroughly. Being in the passenger seat, L.C. clearly saw the driver. She was young and dressed in out-of-day clothing. The style was circa 1940, as it looked to him. She was even wearing a fur coat, and had on a feathered hat.

Beside her sat a child. Whether female or male was a matter of conjecture, because the child had on a thick coat and hat, as well. All this heavy clothing was curious under the circumstances, because although cool out, it wasn't chilly L.C. and his associate, "Charlie," had all the windows down. For them, it was a lovely autumn day to enjoy.

Then something curious happened. As they proceeded to pass the vehicle, the woman looked panicked, frightened in the extreme. She twisted her head left and right, her glance darting frantically here and there. To "L.C." and "Charlie," it looked as if she were lost or in some sort of distress.

At this point, L.C. called out to her, inquiring if she was in need of any sort of aid. The woman gave an emphatic nod of her head. In response, he gestured for her to stop. He did this several times, trying to get his message across to her, for conversation of more than a word or so was difficult with her windows tightly shut, as if against cold weather.

She finally nodded. However, she now wore a quizzical expression when she looked over at them, as if confused by the sight of either them, their vehicle, or both. Finally, she did as he gestured for her to do, and she slowed down and began pulling over to the right side of the road.

At this point, the two men pulled ahead of her, and then slowed, stopping in front of her car along the shoulder...or so they thought. Turning to look back, even as they began climbing out of their own vehicle, they saw nothing. The antique car, along with the woman and child in it, had vanished. The highway was empty in either direction except for one approaching car. This stretch had been a straight one. There were no curves or hills for a retreating vehicle to have disappeared around or behind. In short, the antique car had just disappeared without a trace and there was simply no way it could have conceivably done so.

They simply stood there, stunned, as the approaching car pulled over. The driver leapt out of the vehicle and ran up to them. Without any sort of preamble, he just started demanding to know where the other car had gone. He, too, had seen it. Moreover, his testimony as a reliable witness also adds to the credence of this strange tale.

The driver declared later that he, too, had been traveling only the same highway. Ahead of him, he saw a normal-looking car start to pace an antique model, but at such a low rate of speed, as to nearly have come to a halt while doing so. He had slowed accordingly.

Then, he watched as the newer car passed back into the lane in front of the ancient vehicle. At this point, the antique hid the new car from sight. Then, abruptly, the old car disappeared. The new man had pulled over to the side of the road and stopped. Of the antique car, there was now no sign at all.

Struggling to find a reason for the car disappearing so suddenly, he wondered if there had been some sort of accident during the passing, if the car somehow been bumped and so had gone out of control and off the road into a hidden ditch. Nevertheless, there was no sign of any accident having happened, no wrecked car in sight anywhere.

Not content to let the matter immediately drop, all three men remained there, searching the sides of the road, but to no avail. They found nothing. The newer arrival felt they should all report the incident, but both L.C. and Charlie, declined to do this.

After all, what could they tell the police that was even believable—that they'd seen an antique car with a woman and child dressed in out-of-date clothes suddenly disappear in plain sight? They felt that no one would believe and they were almost certainly right in thinking this.

Without their support and corroboration of his story, the newer arrival felt that he, too, couldn't report the incident, not on his own. However, they did give each other's contact information and for a long time after that, they kept in communication, even talking on the telephone with one another on occasion. They rehashed the incident repeatedly, but there was no new information and eventually they fell out of contact as a result.

Was this a ghost? That answer seems unlikely. The details are too vivid, too well described by all observers of the event. Moreover, the woman interacted with L.C. and Charlie. She responded to them when they communicated with her. There is also the matter of her looking scared and "lost," as the two men had described her. It was as if she, too, felt something strange was going on. Then there is the matter of the third witness who viewed the whole event from a different perspective, from behind as he approached them. The car looked just as real to him, as well. That is...until it disappeared.

**Event Summary:** Based on the witness accounts, the number of them and their seeming reliability, something strange does seem to have really taken place on that fateful day. Furthermore, it has all the hallmarks other reported time travel experiences have. There seems to be a remarkable consistency in these tales, the very "realness" of them, the clear and detailed descriptions, as well as often there being interactions with these people from other times.

Ghosts, it would seem, would hardly be likely to pull over to the side of the road in their ghost cars at the request of strangers, or so one would think. Therefore, this does seem to have been a time travel event of some sort or other.

**English Couples' Trip To The Past.** This strange story follows a similar pattern to many other such ones. The year was 1989 and two couples from the United Kingdom were on holiday on the Continent. At one point, while traveling through a rural area of France, it started to get late, so they began looking for a hotel to stop at overnight.

Although not having been in the area before, they distinctly remembered it later on, for there had been announcements for a circus posted on signs at various locations along the way. The circus, judging from the illustrations, looked distinctly like something from another era, one long gone by. However, in France at the time, circuses were still popular, so none of the foursome thought too much about this aspect of things. Besides, who knew how long the signs had been up? They could have been for years.

Eventually, the foursome came to an inn, where some locals loitering out front of the place advised them of a hotel being a little farther on down the road. This hotel, they then proceeded to find. Upon reaching it, the place appeared antiquated to them and certainly was by the more modern standards of the late 1980s. Made mostly of wood and lacking anything of a contemporary nature in the way of accoutrements, such as phones, etc., and like the circus scenes depicted in the signs they had passed earlier, the hotel seemed terribly out of date. Still, it was getting late and they were tired. They felt they had little choice but to stay. For one night, the place would do, they supposed.

They spent an uneventful night there. Next morning, two gendarmes, French police officers, came into the reception area of the hotel. The two couples were surprised by the outfits they wore, for they, too, seemed terribly out of date, even having capes attached to them. Still, the two officers seemed nice enough and even gave them directions on how to continue their journey. After paying a remarkably cheap bill for the night, the foursome left the hotel and set out on their trip once more.

The two couples enjoyed the next two weeks of their vacation, touring about southern Europe. However, eventually, their time was up and so they had to head home for the United Kingdom. Traveling through the same region of France, they felt it might be fun once again to stay at the same, old-fashioned hotel. After all, it certainly had been affordable. Additionally, it was pretty countryside, with nothing seeming to have changed their much in decades. As they approached the area, even the circus signs were still there, still undisturbed, as they might have been for years and years.

However, there was a problem. Try as they might, they could not locate the hotel. Although they were sure they were in the right place, on the right road, given the circus signs and all, the hotel simply was not there.

The foursome were bewildered. How could this be? Something that looked as if it had been there, perhaps for over a century or more, was completely missing. There was no sign of it at all. To compound the mystery, the foursome later discovered that not only did their photographs taken while at the hotel not develop, but on later investigation, also that French police hadn't worn such style of caped outfits since the turn of the century. Ultimately, they had no choice but to continue their journey home.

**Summary of Event:** The foursome were adamant about this event having happened. They were utterly convinced that this odd incident had really taken place. Nonetheless, without any sort of photographic evidence to support their case, the story simply faded away over time. Yet, the two couples always remained convinced ever after that they had somehow traveled back in time to stay at a hotel that had existed in the late 1800s, only to have it later disappear, never to be found by them or anyone else again.

Time travel incidents don't only include just those of the past, as we've seen with Sir Robert Goddard and the pilot, Bruce Gernon. They also involve future time events, as well and sometimes in amazing ways. For example:

**A Chilling Look At A Future War.** J. Bernard Hutton, along with photojournalist, Joachim Brandt, had to complete a piece on the major shipyard of Germany situated in Hamburg. This was in 1932, years before World War II started (1939). Their assignment was to do a complete workup on the shipyard, including taking photos, doing interviews, etc.

They arrived in Germany without incident and proceeded to accomplish their mission. This also happened without incident. However, that abruptly and drastically changed as they started to leave the shipyard behind them, now thinking their job was done and so they could head on home.

First, there came the sound of airplanes, and it was as if there were many, all flying in a mass formation above the shipyard. Surprised by this, they attempted to determine what type of planes they were.

One has to remember that this was well before Hitler had Goring build up the German air force, the Luftwaffe, so this number of planes, ones sufficient to create such a loud noise, was a real mystery at the time. Under the treaty of Versailles ending WWI, the Germans shouldn't have had anywhere near so many military aircraft.

Moreover, Hitler didn't even seize total control of Germany until January of the following year, 1933. So again, so many planes presented a real enigma. The two men halted their trip from the shipyard to get a closer look at the approaching aircraft.

They mystery turned to shock. Bombs started to fall. Explosions sounded. According to the two men, the whole area seemed engulfed in flames as fuel storage facilities exploded. Buildings blew apart, while others crumpled in on themselves. Machinery shattered into pieces. In short, the much vaunted and famed Hamburg Shipyard was under a full enemy attack and suffering major destruction in the form of bombs raining from the mystery planes above.

The two men were stunned, to say the least, and at a loss as to what to do. One mutual thought occurred to them and that was to seek safety. They piled into their vehicle and sped toward the gate of the shipyard, intent on trying to leave at least the worst of the affected area behind them, if only in order to survive. As they went, defensive antiaircraft weapons began to fire, and this surprised them, as well, for they had seen no sign of such weaponry upon their arrival. Pausing at the gate only for a brief moment to inquire if they could be of any help, the guard ordered them to proceed to safety. This they did and as quickly as they could. Nonetheless, they had been smart enough to take photographs of the event, or so they thought.

As they made their way back to Hamburg proper, a strange change occurred. The dark sky over the shipyard was not visible over the city. There, everything was normal and bright. Moreover, nobody seemed alarmed. People went about their business in the usual fashion, and there was no sign of any attack there, nothing to denote the terrible devastation occurring just miles away from the metropolis. Everything seemed normal and peaceful, too much so.

At this point, bewildered by this strange contrast of things, they decided to pause in their trip to look back toward the shipyard. The two men were determined to try to figure out just what was going on, how all this could be. To their amazement, the shipyard looked just fine. There it was in the distance with no sign of the incredible and fierce aerial attack. No buildings blazed in the distance. There was nothing in the way of smoke. Furthermore, of the enemy airplanes, nothing was now visible. Moreover, even there, the sky wasn't dark area anymore. All seemed perfectly normal.

Nor did the surprises for them stop coming. Upon later developing the photographs Brandt had managed to take, including ones he had continued to take during the attack and their subsequent flight, nothing seemed unusual, wrong, or out-of-place in any of them. The shipyard in all the pictures looked just fine. Buildings were intact. Cranes still stood, and of the hail of fire from the sky, there was no sign in any of the photographs of such a thing ever having occurred.

Upon returning home, they told their editor of the event. However, without photographic evidence to support their bizarre contentions, nothing came of it. Instead, the editor felt he was the victim of some practical joke, or perhaps the men were intoxicated, but actually believing in their story? No, he absolutely did not.

Years later, after the outbreak of WWII, Hutton chanced upon a London newspaper account of a bombing raid on the Hamburg Shipyard. The photos in the article showed a devastated place, one struck exactly as he and Brandt had seen it happen on their trip there back in 1932, seven years before the war even began…

**Event Summary:** This sort of thing is actually typical of events that seem to be time travel occurrences. Often, machinery, such as cameras, do not capture what the people see. This makes one wonder if the witnesses involved are somehow seeing the event in such a way that cameras can't be useful, as with perhaps the observers receiving the imagery in some sort of psychic way. Nonetheless, these two men had managed to see what they did at the Hamburg dockyards, and it shook them to their core. The episode had frightened them considerably, and left them wondering for the rest of their lives not just what they had seen, but how they could have seen it at all. They had watched a war occurring years before it its actual time.

**Another Trip To The Future Or Another Timeline?** Four, young, female students of Southern Utah University experienced what they claim to be a trip to the future, and a most unusual one at that. This was in 1972.

The foursome was making the return trip from Pioche, Nevada, back to their university residences in Cedar City, Utah. Like most universities of the time, there was a curfew, one for which they couldn't be late, or face serious repercussions if they were.

Their journey took them along Highway 56 and here is where the story begins to become strange right at the outset. The highway had long had an unsettling stigma attached to it as being a weird and sinister one. Stories of strange events had circulated for years about the road among the locals.

However, the young women weren't concerned about this negative status of the highway upon which they traveled at the time, being only intent on getting to Cedar City in a timely manner. Already, it was ten o'clock and so they were anxious. The clock was definitely ticking for them.

Coming to a division in the highway, they had to decide whether to travel north or south. They chose north. After traveling a while on this section of road, the surface switched from tarmac to concrete. This made them wonder if they'd taken a wrong turn, since none of them remembered any stretch of concrete road on Highway 56 so far from any town.

They became amazed and truly concerned when the highway then came to an abrupt finish at the base of a towering cliff. Now, they felt certain they had gone the wrong way. Panicking, knowing they would be late if they didn't hurry, they turned around and headed back the way they had come, intent on retracing their route.

Worse was to come. Now, the countryside looked different from on their trip north. Here, there was a rough terrain of canyons and red-earth gullies. These were more reminiscent of Sedona, Arizona, than this area of Utah and so seemed wildly out of place to them.

Finally, as they continued their strange journey, these began to turn to smooth fields of wheat or grain. There were pines, as well. The problem was that none of the young women remembered this sort of landscape being anywhere near Cedar City, either, or even in this section of the state, for that matter. Everything had acquired a decidedly unfamiliar look to it.

More panicked than ever by this state of affairs, and worried much less about the curfew and now much more about what was happening to them, it was with real relief when they spotted signs of civilization ahead. They saw a bar alongside the highway. Reaching it, they pulled into the parking area. One of the foursome called through her open window to several men, wanting to find out from them just where they were and to get directions on how to get back to Cedar City.

However, while things had just seemed weird to the four students before this point, now they became truly frightening. The young woman pulled her head back from the open window and shouted at the top of her lungs for their driver to get them out of there, immediately. Hearing the urgency and terror in her friend's voice, the girl driving their car, did as ordered.

She whipped the car around and back onto the highway. It was then they saw they were being followed, the men having given chase to them by getting into their own vehicle, which was, as they later described it, an "egg-shaped" one with just three wheels, like a tricycle.

They raced down the highway, intent of fleeing the strange men and their strange vehicle. At one point, seeming to have outpaced the car following them, they also realized the landscape had once again become more familiar to them. The road they travelled was now the one they recognized as Highway 56.

When then asked why she had been so alarmed by the fact of seeing the men, the student told the other young women the men, as she put it, "hadn't been "human." They had been something else. They continued on their way to Cedar City without further incident.

There is actually much more detail to this story, an in-depth account of it all, but this suffices for our purposes here and gives us the gist of what happened. If you wish to read the longer and more detailed account, please see the links in the section titled *"References"* at the end of this book.

**Conclusion:** I must interject a personal note here in the form of my own opinion and it is just my opinion. The strange vehicle does sound like it could be a future version of our automobiles of today, and so the young women conceivably could have traveled into the future.

However, two other factors seem to make this explanation less likely for me. First, the landscape changed dramatically on their trip, was very unfamiliar to them. The geological nature of it had altered. Unless the four students had catapulted quite far into the future, which is conceivable perhaps, this would not be the case. Landscapes with canyons and hills erode only slowly compared to the human time scale of things. It takes many thousands of years for such to happen usually, at the very least. Consequently, if they went into the future of our world, it had to have been a very long way, indeed!

Secondly, the fact the "men" weren't human also is an oddity. Did the students travel so far into the future that humans were no longer human, or something else had entirely supplanted them by then? This is possible, as most things are, of course.

Yet, the fact they were at a tavern of sorts does sound oddly human-like. It is not what one would necessarily expect from some other advanced and very different species, one having supplanted us in the far future. Could it still be possible, the idea of the young women having a forward trip in time?

Again, yes of course, it could. Nevertheless, it is just how possible the likelihood of this might be that bothers me. I just don't find it very likely. If the creatures weren't human, just what were they? One has to ask this question. Moreover, why were they so human-like in some ways, what with taverns, parking lots, highways, etc.?

Therefore, with these oddly similar aspects, but with the different landscapes and/or terrain, and the strange "men," it does make one wonder if this was our actual future or perhaps a different timeline entirely. Could it have been a parallel world? Was this a timeline where humans didn't exist and never had, but something sort of like us did? At least, if they did, they looked considerably different from us, it seems.

This would then account for a road forking, being made of concrete instead of asphalt, and their dead-ending at a cliff. It would also explain, as well, the strange nature of the terrain, and the "men," if the young women somehow had transferred to a different timeline other than ours. After all, they might have their own version of our highways "over there," but ones designed differently, and meant to accommodate a different sort of terrain and so a different type of vehicle, as well. Hence, the roads might well be concrete instead of just asphalt.

Furthermore, the fact that locals for a long time thought the highway haunted is also an interesting point here. If there were trans-time phenomenon occurring in the area, causing shifts in time, and whether to the future, past, or to parallel timelines, this could easily account for the tales of the highway being haunted. If temporary crossovers to other timelines were happening on a regular basis to people, this would certainly give rise to such beliefs about that road.

People would claim to see strange things, of course. When combined, the different terrain, highways, "men," and type of vehicle, again, for me personally, this seems to have been a trip to a different timeline, a parallel universe, rather than our own future.

Therefore, where the two men who had gone to Hamburg do seem to have had a vision of a future event, one years ahead of their own time, the young women seem to have traveled a very different sort of road (pun intended). Although, they, too, might have gone into the future, it would seem more likely, given their descriptions of the incident, that they somehow crossed over to another reality for a while. It was a reality so different from ours that humans as we know them did not exist.

# CHAPTER 6
# Time Machines?

*"Time travel is such a magic concept."*
— Matt Smith, Time Lord, *Doctor Who?*

**Are Time Machines Real?** We've all heard of time machines in science fiction. Whether it is the marvelous steampunk type used in H.G. Well's, *Time Machine*, or the blue, police-box Tardis of the television series, *Doctor Who*, they are marvelous inventions, indeed. Of course, these are just pieces of fiction, and at times, rather wild fiction at that. Right?

Maybe not. One thing that may surprise many people is the idea of real time machines already existing, and by this, I don't mean in the future, but right in the here and now. People are either actually working on building time machines, or as some rumors persist in saying, have already done so.

**A Professor Wants To Save His Dead Father**. Remember, we mentioned Professor Ron Mallet in passing earlier, under the section on just how time travel might be able to work? As also mentioned, he is actively pursuing the creation of a time machine. We will discuss this here now in more depth. The idea was that the device might be able to send at least information, if not objects, back through time.

This is an intriguing idea of his. Still, in a world where science still looks doubtfully at such things, still persists in tending to ridicule those who actually try to invent such a thing, why is he, a well-credentialed professor, so insistent and tenacious in trying to achieve this goal?

The truth of this, as most truths are, is simple and yet profound. He lost his beloved father at an early age. As Professor Mallet himself has said in a number of interviews, he dreamed of being able to invent a time machine so he could go back in time and somehow alter events, and save his father.

Haven't we all wished to do this with someone at some time in our lives? Well, unlike the rest of us, Ron Mallet is actually trying to achieve this goal. He uses the following equation as the basis to try to realize this dream. The equation is included here not for you to try to understand it in any sort of detail, but to simply show how simple and elegant a thing it is.

Perhaps what Einstein's elegant and simple E=MC² did for the Theory of Special Relativity; Theoretical Physicist Ron Mallet's simple formula can do for time travel. Instead of some blackboard full of esoteric and enigmatic formulas scrawling rune-like all over the place, Professor Mallet has this simple formula (well, relatively simple…):

$$\dot{\Omega} = \frac{8\sqrt{2}\, G\rho}{ac^3}$$

Again, it isn't necessary to state here what each symbol stands for, since this book isn't a course in higher mathematics or theoretical physics, for that matter. Rather, the idea here is just to show how simple and short the formula for possible time travel really is! (If you would like a more in-depth look at the above formula, learn more about it all, and the work of Professor Ron Mallet, please see the representative links for this under "*References*.")

The idea behind Professor Mallet's approach, which he is already hard at work at trying to prove in reality, is a simple one in its most basic form. The equation shows how if one warps space, or rather causes it to "twist" with the use of a laser, there are some interesting results. If a particle, in this case, he uses a neutron, travels along into this twisting of space, then the same must hold true for time, as well.

He bases this idea on Einstein's theory that space isn't just space, but that space and time are integral parts of the same phenomenon, and thus is "spacetime." Accordingly, if you twist space, you are twisting spacetime.

Moreover, the conclusion to this idea is then equally simple; the neutron moves along into not only the twist in space, but also the resulting twist in time. In short, the neutron would travel through time.

Again, Professor Mallet's famous analogy is that of a cup of coffee. Stir a cup of coffee and drop something into it that floats, as with a small foam bead, for example. The bead will start to spin around along with the stirred coffee in the cup, and just as a neutron would spin if in a "spacetime" stirred by a laser.

Really get the coffee swirling with that spoon (the substitute for the laser in this example), and you start to get a whirlpool effect at the center, a real twisting of the coffee there, a vortex. Spacetime can twist just like this, as well, according to the current theories of physics.

Just as a foam bead spins around in a loop in the little whirlpool in the center of the coffee cup, the neutron particle can swirl around in a complete loop in spacetime, as well. If the laser light can manage it, "stir" spacetime enough, the neutron is carried along, or "frame-dragged" along until it loops back in time.

The catch here is that the neutron, like the foam bead floating in the cup of coffee, couldn't go back further in time than the start of the stirring process itself. It could only loop back as far as the beginning of that process, but no further.

Again, so sure is Professor Ron Mallet about all this, that he has been raising money and has already been starting experiments to see if this will work. If it does, we will have our first true time machine that can take something back in time!

In this case, we are talking about particles. Nevertheless, a stream of particles could encode information in them. If this is possible, then information could conceivably go back in time. Again, the caveat here is that such information could not go back before someone creates the time machine. Even so, this would certainly prove a tremendous achievement, to send information back in time! If we had such a device up and running for a few decades, that means information from a future time, ten, twenty, thirty or more years from now, could be sent back to us in the here and now. We could actually get messages from the future!

There are other rumors about existing time machines, as well. Some of them seem to have real substance to them. The following is a case in point.

**The Strange Case Of "Sid" Hurwich.** Here we have the odd case of an appliance repairman who lived in Canada. As a child, Sid was a bit strange. He was incredibly fascinated, some might say even obsessively fixated, on machinery. He would scavenge bits and pieces and then create actual working devices from such random parts.

This was no simple little hobby, because as an adult, Sid became famous for his talent at repairing just about any sort of appliance. In fact, in his home city of Toronto, he became legendary for this. Sid became so good at what he could do, that at one point, a power company was instrumental in getting Sid out of serving in the military so that he could aid them in setting up an electrical grid system.

Now, the story gets strange. Being a virtual genius at what he could do, Sid made a good deal of money very early on his life. When he became a victim of a heart attack at the low age of 36, he retired, having made enough money already comfortably to do so. This money also allowed him to continue working at his own, and now slower speed, on any projects he wished to do.

Being born in 1918, and having grown up in the early part of the 20th Century, Sid lived in a time when many things seemed popular and there were few legal restrictions to forbid people working on pretty much whatever they wanted to, even if it sometimes could be dangerous.

It's said that at this time, he managed to create not so much a time machine (although one supposes it still fits the definition of one), as a machine that could alter time sufficienctly to "freeze it."

This thing could also affect machinery within a certain radius around it. Whether this was a sideffect of freezing time, or a separate function remains unclear even to this day.

What is clearer is that a series of bank robberies plagued the city of Toronto in 1969. At this point, Sid told the police he could aid them with his machine. He could cause time to freeze and so the police could then find out what had happened, how the robberies had taken place in detail.

An article in a British Columbia newspaper stated that Sid Hurwich demonstrated the time-freezing device to the police at his home. One of the officers stated that when the device was activated, he couldn't raise his weapon from the table. It was as if it was frozen in place there. Moreover, he couldn't pull the trigger on the gun, either. It wouldn't move.

At this point in the proceedings, Sid told the officers to check their watches. They were off the current time by 25 minutes, apparently also having been frozen in time by the effect of Sid's device. Supposedly, as the officers left the home, Sid's wife overhead one of them comment about the possible military applications of such a device as Sid had created. This is all according to an account published in the *Vancouver Sun Times*.

We're not finished. Here the story gets even stranger yet, because later, the military application might just have actually happened. Sid was Jewish and attended the synagogue of Besh Tzedec in Toronto. Later in his life, Sid was given an award there. This was the Protectors of the State Of Israel Award, and was from the Zionist Orgaization of Canada.

The story goes that it was for a mysterious device which he had donated to the Israeli military some seven years prior to getting the award, and that the device had somehow been instrumental in the famous "Raid on Entebbe," of July 4, 1976, which was later to be the subject of not just one, but two movies.

This raid rescued many trapped Israelites from where they were being kept hostage in Uganda. The event had been a stunning success. The newspaper, the *Toronto Star*, made this link or connection in a published article some weeks after Sid Hurwich was given the award. However, the story was picked up and sent worldwide, and so was republished in some reliable sources, being published in the *Economist Magazine* in the United Kingdom, as well.

The report stated that somehow, a device created by Sid Hurwich, was apparently capable of altering the center of gravity, as well as nearby magnetic fields, thus interfering with mechanical, as well as electronic devices within the radius of effect. The device did this by emitting some sort of "beams." References have been made to this as being very similar in nature to the legendary "Tesla Shield," supposedly invented or at least designed by Nicolai Tesla. How similar they really are is unknown.

Now all this may seem highly implausible, but remember, this was not a "crackpot." Sid Hurwich started not just one, but two successful companies. One was SidCo Company and the other was Shock Electric, and that is still a going and successful concern. So the man wasn't some "fly-by-night" nut-case, but rather far from it!

How true is the actual story? Well, the newspaper accounts seem to back it up, as does his receiving an award. There is no doubt they gave him one, so that part of it, at least, is true. So this in itself is pretty telling, and shows that something serious had been going on.

However, whether or not the time freezing device existed or was actually used in the Entebbe raid by the Israeli military is much harder to verify. This is especially true since it's all supposed to be top secret. All we have to go on are two bouts of newspaper reports at two very different times.

Still, if the device did not exist, or was not used (and apparently if used, it worked very successfully), why was Sid given such a prestigious award by the Israelis if he hadn't been of a great help to them in some secret way? He had to have done something fairly impressive to earn such a thing.

But what? There seems nothing else he could have done. He was too old to go on the raid himself by far at that point. He was not a strategist and had almost no military background, so of what other use could he have been to the military?

Nothing was stated at the ceremony as to why he achieved such an honor, why they had decided to give him the medal in the first place, which was also strange, as if it were truly meant it to be kept a secret and not ever made public. Again, not giving a reason for such an honor is, in itself, very odd.

Did Sid Hurwich actually build a time device that could freeze time in some way? It seems very possible he just might have. We have tantalizing clues, some reasonable evidence this may, in fact, be just what happened. Yet, we don't have a smoking gun, as the saying goes.

Perhaps someday, we will know for sure. If the Israeli powers-that-be ever decide to allow the full story to become public, to share it with the world, the truth may finally become known. In any case, why

Sid would receive such an award otherwise remains a complete and compelling mystery, an enigma of no small proportions. If not for a time machine that could freeze time, even as the police had reported years before, then just what was the award for?

**Sid Hurwich and His Special Award**

**Large Hadron Collider A Time Machine?** For a long time, laypersons have referred to such particle colliders as "atom smashers." This is an apt description, because such colliders do smash atomic particles together at incredibly high speeds (almost the speed of light) to see what comes out of those collisions. This is how we discover new subatomic particles.

However, the term "atom smasher" doesn't do the Large Hardon Collider justice. For one thing, the collider is the most intricate machine ever built by humanity (that we, the public, are aware of, at least). The complexity of the Large Hadron Collider, and even its size (mostly underground), is astonishing. The collider creates a 17-mile circle in circumference and crosses the border of Switzerland and France in order to do this.

Scientists designed the Large Hadron Collider specifically to smash together protons, head on, at incredible speeds and with immense force. To get an idea of how powerful these collisions are, a number of people, members of the general public, but some scientists, as well, were (and some still are) afraid such collisions might result in the creation of mini black holes, or possibly even wormholes. Some even worried it might cause "tears" in the very fabric of our universe that might ultimately lead to its total destruction. Luckily, this hasn't happened, at least, not yet...

Among the several monumental discoveries the collider has already allowed us to make is that of the Higgs Boson, a fundamental particle of the universe, often referred to as the "God Particle," so important is it.

What does this have to do with time travel? Well, some theorize the Higgs boson might be instrumental in creating another particle, the Higgs singlet. A researcher at Vanderbilt University, Professor Tom Weiler and his colleague Chui Man Ho, theorize that such a particle would have some odd capabilities, and that these in no way would defy the laws of quantum physics as they are now known.

In short, they think that among the properties of the theoretical Higgs singlet might be the particle's ability to transit to the fifth dimension. In this dimension, the Higgs singlet would be quite capable of moving through time, both into the future, as well as the past! If this is so, it will mean the discovery of a real time-traveling particle!

**Conclusion:** As we can see here in this chapter, time machines are not just stuff meant for the realms of fantasy and/or science fiction. Real people are working on real time machines and various concepts for time travel. Famous physicists and others have pushed the frontiers incredibly far in just the last few decades.

We have renowned scientists attempting to create time travel by stirring spacetime with a laser. We have others who already may have built time machines, as with the one that freezes time (Sid Hurwich). We have particles that just might also exist that travel through time, as with the Higgs singlet, or perhaps even the neutrino in some instances, the so-called "ghost particle." Therefore, the idea of time machines being just the product of a vivid imagination is now truly an outmoded concept. Time machines, it seems, may soon exist if they don't already…

# CHAPTER 7
# Time Traveler Anachronisms In History

*If time travel is possible, where are the tourists from the future?*
— Stephen Hawking, *A Brief History of Time*

The quotation above is a very telling one, is it not? It is also a rather condemning one, because if Professor Hawking were right, one would expect time travelers, if they have been popping in and out of history on a regular basis to leave an impression of some sort, at least, something that noticeable to some extent.

Of course, Stephen Hawking, a noted physicist and cosmologist of unbelievable high repute, is being just a bit tongue-in-cheek here, although his point is still serious enough. After all, one would hardly expect time travelers to materialize in midtown New York wearing silver lamé shirts and shorts, complete with silver socks and shoes and wearing some type of 3D holographic camera slung around their necks.

As much as we might wish they would be that obvious for us to see, like some Americans on holiday in Europe or elsewhere are, for instance (and believe me, we are obvious to the locals at times…), that just probably wouldn't be the case.

Still, Stephen is right. We should have seen signs they have been here, have "fooled around" with the past. So why don't we? Well, here is another quotation that could well answer Stephen Hawking's one and quite well:

*"When a traveler from the future must talk, he does not talk but whimpers. He whispers tortured sounds. He is agonized. For if he makes the slightest alteration in anything, he may destroy the future...."*

— **Alan Lightman, *Einstein's Dreams***

That quotation also makes sense, doesn't it, at least just as much as Stephen Hawking's might? Furthermore, it would be an excellent reason why time travelers don't stick out like the proverbial "sore thumb" as Stephen Hawking would seem to imply they should. Maybe, just maybe, they are here, but don't dare show themselves for fear of altering the timeline they are visiting, and thus their own future time. Nobody wants to accidentally pop out of existence through some silly little error, as it were.

If this is true, it does make for a good answer to physicist, Stephen Hawking's question. Yet, would we not see *something* if time travelers were visiting various times and places in the past, some sort of results and/or effects of their visits? Shouldn't there be some indication of their having been there, some sort of lasting effect or influence to some small degree, at least?

These are reasonable questions, after all. Additionally, to answer them, yes, we probably should see something like this if time travelers don't care about changing our timeline too much. However, would we, ourselves, see the results here in our timeline if this happened?

Again, the answer is yes. This would be so even if the theory put forward by a number of quantum physicists that if one travels back in time and makes an alteration there, then that creates a new and branching timeline from that point forward. It would cause a split or fork in the original timeline. There would be a new branching timeline. It would contain the change and so would mean a new and alternate future. Yet, the time traveler's own timeline would remain unaffected, it still being on the original timeline. Only the new and branching reality would contain the changes.

Therefore, changing things in the past for the time traveler would be no problem, not for them, at least! For the rest of us, the consequences might be very different, perhaps more severe and much longer lasting, meaning forever... This is a very neat theory, because it means that if one travels back into the past and changes something, one's own future is still quite safe, and remains unaltered. Moreover, if that time traveler journeyed again back into the past to alter the same event yet another and different way, and no matter how many times he might do this, all he ends up doing is creating more alternate timelines.

Still, if this is the case, if time travelers can safely affect changes, then we are once more back to Stephen Hawking's question; where are they, these insidious travelers from the future who wantonly change our timeline? Why don't we see these time traveling "tourists?"

There could be a number of reasonable causes for the lack of them:

**1.** Maybe, the physicists are wrong and traveling through time does affect the traveler's own future time, so to do so is a very dangerous thing to accomplish safely. Therefore, only on a very rare basis and only after careful consideration and with the strictest controls, might such time travel happen. That is, if it is dared to be done at all. A brilliant science fiction story based on this idea, *A Sound Of Thunder,* by author, Ray Bradbury, explores this idea and does so very well. (The movie version is not nearly as good, in my personal opinion.)

**2.** Time travel could be very difficult to accomplish, even for our future descendants, or those post-human "others" who might be trying to do the deed. They effort could require complex technology and massive amounts of energy, even equivalent to that of a supernova, as some physicists conjecture. Therefore, there would be few trips to the past, so few of those annoying time traveling tourists to mess things up, for us to notice, or to make any sort of impact on our history.

**3.** Time travel could be expensive, perhaps incredibly so, and current knowledge of physics suggests this might be the case, so this, too, could act as a real brake on the number of time travel trips made. A future government might be the only institution capable of paying for such a costly thing. Therefore, this could be why time travelers might be very few in numbers.

Therefore, time travel could well be rather be like the fact that most people simply can't afford a trip around the world, even if they can make it to nearby Florida and Disney World. It might be possible for them to do this much, but just too expensive for most people to accomplish traveling farther afield.

It is only the very rich, for instance, who have signed up for flights into space on the upcoming commercial ventures into this realm. Moreover, despite the number of wealthy in the world, we are just talking a small handful of them, really, who have committed to going.

**4.** Time travel might be only in some sort of governmental hands, under strict governmental controls of some sort. This, too, would limit those pesky, time-traveling tourists to a large degree. Where a time traveler would go, how long they could stay there, and what they could accomplish would thus be severely limited and restricted, as well, no doubt, if one goes by current government-run projects of today.

Again, this would mean little interaction with people in the past, much less impact on us with changes to our timeline. Therefore, evidence of time travelers having been in our past or present would be minimal, at best. Instead of thousands taking package-deal trips to the past, there might only be the very few for this reason, perhaps no more than a few.

**5.** Another possibility that might interfere with time travelers popping up all over our timeline is the laws of physics involved in the process, as well. Some scientists argue that the closer to the recent past one tries to travel the more resistance, and so the more energy it might take to accomplish the trip.

Just going back to yesterday might then be hideously costly and difficult to do, again, might take the energy of a supernova star, while going to the very ancient past might not, comparatively speaking, take nearly so much energy. Under these circumstances, we couldn't expect time travelers to have left evidence in our recent past, or even our recorded history, for that matter.

Such "chrononauts" might be restricted to only going back well beyond our time, perhaps even having to travel to such primeval periods as when the dinosaurs lived, or perhaps even further back.

Accordingly, we can see there are quite a number of reasons why we might not have evidence for those pesky time travelers littering up our timeline.

However, let's now suppose sometime in the distant future that time travel has not only become easy, but cheap, as well, and so time traveling is a (relatively) commonplace occurrence. Again, we are back to Stephen Hawking's question of where are they once more, if this is so?

Well, it would appear they are here, of have been at points in the past. Again, a bold statement and one that requires proof. So is there evidence for this? Oh, yes, and I'm not just talking about people claiming to have interacted with such visitors to our time. There is more evidence and some of it is literally hard evidence for something or someone having made trips into our past and even the distant past.

What is this evidence and how do we find it? There are a number of ways:

**1.** We could look for events or incidents in our past that seems unduly strange by normal historical circumstances, truly out of place and odd. In other words, they shouldn't have happened. Moreover, if these events happen more than once in the same way, that could well be another sign.

**2.** We can look for objects the time travelers might have left behind, again hard evidence they might have passed this way at some point, recently or in the far past.

**3.** We can look for singular alterations in the flow of historical events and ones that have been the result of glaring interference. We might just find instances where someone overtly and obviously was messing with our history, for example.

Strangely, we do have evidence of all these things. First, there is the truly ancient and even more recent evidence provided by Oopart objects. As discussed in several of my other books, Oopart is the name given by archaeologists to any object discovered that seems totally out of place for the time it was discovered to have been in.

As an obvious example, if an archaeologist unearthed a car in a dig dating back to the times of the Old Kingdom in ancient Egypt, this would be a wonderful example of an Oopart discovery. In addition, yes, we have many examples of these sorts of things from our past, if not exactly such antiquated automobiles.

We won't go into detail here, because again, I discuss Oopart in depth in several of my other books, but just as a brief overview, here are just some quick examples of Oopart discoveries by not only archaeologists, but others, as well. It is important to remember that these aren't all recent finds by any means. People have unearthed many Oopart objects and items over the last centuries, and not just the last few decades.

**Oopart objects include:**

**1.** Metal ladles, metal vases, a hand bell, a cube of polished and machined metal, a kettle, a hammer, quarrying tools and other tools, many nails, as well as highly machined nano-screws made of various metals. These include those made of titanium alloys, which only more recently has become possible to smelt, requiring very high temperatures to process.

These are just a few of many more such objects found. In addition and as stated earlier, people have unearthed these things at various times throughout the last several centuries and this, around the world. Almost as soon as the science of archaeology and industrial-scale mining both got underway, such strange artifacts began to be unearthed in numbers.

By all rights, some of these objects must date back millions of years, for, as with the ladle, kettle, and such, *they were entirely encased in coal*, which means the coal had to form around the objects. This means they aren't just a few millions of years old, *but tens of millions or more years in age!*

Other oopart objects discovered from archaeological sites date back tens of thousands of years. This is back to a time when they just shouldn't have existed, and according to our scientists, principally archaeologists, couldn't have existed.

**2.** Stone maps as with the Map of God or the Creator, which shows in three-dimensional bas relief, no less, an area of the Caucasus Mountains in Russia, and with major terraforming seeming to have been accomplished there, as with the diversion of rivers and dam building in multiple places. The map showed canals, as well.

The map is large, heavy, said to be a portion of a much larger map, and only made by someone who had performed high aerial surveys of the region. The map is composed of three layers of rock. The rock itself dates back an incredibly long time, millions of years, which one would expect. The outermost layer is a clear material that somehow seems bonded to the underlying and "engraved" layer and acts to "protect" the map's features. How "they" accomplished this is also a mystery.

The age of the map, itself, can't be determined, since there is no way to test the true age yet, but only that of the stone composing it. Considering the alterations to the landscape the map shows, though, one must assume the map is at least tens of thousands of years, if not hundreds of thousands of years at the minimum.

The Map of the Creator is also not far from the region depicted where thousands of screws, many of them nano-scaled, were discovered, which must date back anywhere from nine thousand years to much more, since they were found buried along a river's edge and tributary at a considerable depth. For more on all this, a greater detailing of such discoveries, please see the link under *"References"* at the end of this book to *Time Travel: 35 Cases of Time Travel Intrusion*.

The incredible thing about the Map of the Creator is that it implies not only was someone here tens of thousands, even hundreds of thousands or more years ago (millions by some estimates), but that they had a major impact on the region. When one is altering the course of rivers, constructing numerous dams and more, one if virtually changing the area on such a level as to call it terraforming! Whoever was doing this was altering our landscape in the Caucuses in a very big way.

As we see here, there does seem to be evidence for "things" being left behind by possible time travelers. Furthermore, that evidence often comes to us from previously untouched layers of earth, even from actual archaeological dig sites in some instances. What do the archaeologists and experts make of all this?

Nothing! Absolutely nothing. They either think the finds are hoaxes, which sometimes has cast doubt on the reputations of the archaeologists involved who have found some of these things, or they simply ignore the finds altogether.

This last seems to be their main approach, simply to not even consider such finds in any way or fashion, but rather to act as if they just never happened at all. Such oopart finds in mainstream archaeology are always "just anomalies," and therefore, utterly discounted by archaeologists.

The problem with this denial approach, however they choose to do it, is that it ignores a number of things. This includes the fact that if these are hoaxes, they've been going on for centuries. Furthermore, many of the objects found are inexplicable, such as screws made of titanium with some so small as to be nano-sized. How does one hoax that? Additionally, there have just been so many objects found, and again, from all around the world.

Therefore, the world it seems is full of these so-called anomalies, ones whose origins are unknown. How they managed to end up buried at their locations is an enigma. Did someone throw them away, as with the screws? If so, why?

What their use/purpose might have been, and who left them, is a complete mystery. Some lay buried to a depth of forty feet, others less, but still well below the surface. The "screws" in various sizes and alloys are literally in their thousands. Again, if a hoax, that's some hoax!

Therefore, it would seem inconceivable somebody went around and,

1. Made all these special screws in different alloys under difficult conditions at best, and in their thousands, and

2. Then purposely buried them all up and down a river and its tributary, sometimes at considerable depths, as well as over a vast area. Such an endeavor would take a great deal of effort in its own right to accomplish, let alone making the screws to such a tiny scale, of such exotic and various alloys, and so many of them.

In fact, most likely, such a thing isn't possible unless someone on the scale of a major modern corporation specializing in manufacturing such things was involved, or a government was responsible, or both. Moreover, to what purpose would they have done this? There seems to be no rational explanation, none that would suffice.

No, the situation would appear to be that at some time in the far past, these screws were, for whatever reasons, discarded and/or left behind if their creators left this world or that time. The river carried the screws downstream and eventually deposited them at various resting places. Over long years after this, probably several thousand, at least, they silted over. They ended up buried beneath the surface.

Yet, who could possibly have created such things so long ago and why? The titanium-alloy ones are a real mystery. Titanium is very costly, not because of its rarity so much, but because of the difficulty in refining it, and even extracting it from the ore in the first place. Again, it takes very high temperatures, and this wasn't possible, even in small quantities, until about 1875!

So the upshot of all this? It seems "someone" or more than one group lost items throughout history, even in truly prehistoric times. These various items in different times then gradually became buried, as all things seem to do with the passage of years, and in some instances, even had coal and rock subsequently form around them.

If that "someone" was not any of us today, then who was it? We have never had the capabilities, as far as anyone knows, of creating such things so long ago. In fact, many of the items apparently date back to a time well before humans appeared on Earth at all!

Either extraterrestrials a long time ago were leaving such things behind here on Earth, and it's hard to think how they would use a ladle, handbell, or kettle as we would (the items do seem to have been designed for human hands to hold), or time travelers left these things behind them. This is just as one would expect might happen, now on some camping trip or expedition, perhaps, only in these instances, they happened a long time ago.

After all, what expeditions have we humans undertaken in the recent past where we haven't left unnecessary items and/or litter behind, forgotten things, or by accident failed to retrieve some items? Whether the Amazon jungles, the Arctic, or Antarctic, we are very good at discarding items we no longer leave wherever we happen to be even now. We've even left items on the Moon, Mars, Venus, and other planets! Humans tend to be litter bugs, if well-meaning ones at times, it seems. So is it possible, perhaps even probable that time travelers will do the same? Yes, it certainly is.

**Conclusion:** No matter how one wishes to view this sort of information, one thing seems true; there is evidence throughout our recent past, far past, and long before we started recording our past, of anomalous buried objects. These are often artificial and manufactured ones and they are times we simply can't account for in our current view of history through today's ideas in archaeology. Solid artifacts of a mysterious nature surface. There is no doubt of this. We aren't just talking about a few score of them here over the last few decades, either, but literally thousands and over the last several centuries!

Since almost all archaeologists avoid trying to deal with such finds and either call them hoaxes, anomalies, or just plain refuse to consider them at all, then we must seek elsewhere for answers. Again, that the objects exist is not in doubt. That we simply can't explain so many items in conventional terms of history is also a fact. That there are just too many to ignore (unless you happen to be archaeologists with your head buried in the sand), is also true.

So where did the objects come from? Well, either our view of human history is incredibly wrong by a factor of tens of thousands, hundreds of thousands, or even millions of years, or the objects came from "elsewhere." Either someone brought them to Earth from elsewhere, which is certainly possible, or someone brought them back from some future time.

The question we must ask ourselves here is which is it? Is the answer to this riddle extraterrestrials, or time travelers? Well, we need more information, more evidence to try to discern which solution here is the correct one. With this in mind, let's look at some more such evidence now.

# CHAPTER 8

# Time Traveler Intervention in History

*"Most people think time is like a river that flows swift and sure in one direction...I can tell you they are wrong. Time is an ocean in a storm."*

— *Prince of Persia,* **Created by John Mechner**

In reference to a prior chapter quotation in this book by Stephen Hawking, where he wonders where all the time travelers are, the answer seems to be that they have been here and in rather plain sight many times. Furthermore, as mentioned in the chapter quotation here, where it refers to time being like a storm, there is a possibility actual storms might just be a sign of time travelers, as well, under certain conditions, that is. This sounds outrageous at first glance, perhaps, but maybe not after you read the evidence for this idea a littler later on in this book.

If time travelers were jaunting through history, one would assume they have not only been here recently, but in ancient times, as well. So we should find evidence of these trips, right?

Nevertheless, the problem with trying to identify time travelers is they are probably hard to spot, but perhaps not so much as one might think. Even if they aren't running around in silver suits and proclaiming they are time travelers, another way to look at their having been here is by the impact they might have had on our history.

This, too, is difficult to do and for one very good reason: **ANYTHING THAT HAS OCCURRED IN OUR HISTORY, WE AUTOMATICALLY TAKE AS JUST BEING A "NATURAL" PART OF OUR HISTORY, WHETHER IT WAS OR NOT!**

This is very important to understand, because we can't possibly know how things might have been otherwise and before time travelers instituted changes in our timeline, because those original events are no more, wiped out by the new version of events the time travelers' intervention might have caused. Therefore, it is the new version of events that then becomes part of our history, and the version that would then automatically seem "natural" to us. We wouldn't remember the other version because for us, it then never happened.

Nevertheless, we shouldn't give up in finding a way to check for time travelers. Just as astronomers can't see a black hole, because being a black hole, they just aren't visible to us; scientists can still determine they are there by looking at other evidence that tells them of their presence. They look for the effects black holes have on their surroundings. We can do the same with time travelers.

How do we do this? Well, we could:

(1) Look for significant events in history that just seem to go completely contrary to what one would think would happen under normal circumstances, but they would have to be truly critical events, ones that would change the sweep of history forever after. Then, if there were signs of some outside interference (whatever the cause), we might suspect "someone" was behind the critical change in our timeline. Additionally,

(2) We can look for events that just leap out at one from history, as it were. These types of events would be ones for which no "natural," "normal," or simple explanation is available. In short, they are enigmas as to how and why they could have occurred at all.

Do we have any of either types of this sort of evidence? Yes, in fact, we do! There is a lot of it; so sadly, there just isn't room for it all here. However, let's take a quick look at some of the major events that fall into either of these two categories. We'll start in early times and move forward.

One thing to remember to remember here, though; with written records from long ago, there is, of course, the problem of how accurate the accounts might be. Still, if such written accounts have survived for millennia, this is one positive sign they might have been reasonably accurate.

Fairy tales come and go and alter a great deal with time, but written accounts of what people of the times state are real historical events don't seem nearly so subject to this sort of hazy retelling and distortion over the years. Nevertheless, since one must remember that these accounts were often written through the eyes of their religious authors, or people with definite biases, the interpretations they derived from the circumstances of the events (e.g., it was "God's" doing), could well be very biased as a result. For example:

**Jericho.** The story of Joshua taking the City of Jericho is a very interesting one from the time-travel perspective. Joshua led the Israelites into the Promised Land, where they had to take the city of Jericho. This was accomplished only after Joshua was directed (by God, or "someone") to have his troops march around the city for a period of days and each day, and then after all this, do it one more time. They then sounded their trumpets and gave a tremendous shout. The rest is biblical history/legend for the walls "came-a tumblin' down."

Now from a religious standpoint, the story stands as the people recorded it, as an act of God. This was a truly major act of God according to them, and the city did fall, it seems. After all, we have archaeological evidence of the original inhabitants of the region. We have the ruins of Jericho that show it did suffer a disastrous fate and more than once. Therefore, the Bible tale seems to be reasonably on target with this part of the story.

A stranger part of it all is the lack of any mercy at all shown the inhabitants of Jericho, in that the Old Testament also refers to the fact that "God had hardened the hearts" of the inhabitants of the city. This then, meant that Joshua had to order his men to kill them all, not just the men, but the women and children, as well — all of them! Nor was he bidden to stop there. God also ordered Joshua to wipe out all the pets, beasts of burden, and domestic beasts, as well. Nothing at all was to survive — nothing!

How do we account for such a bizarre and horribly cruel act, even by the standards of the day, if it actually took place? In addition, there is strong archaeological evidence to support the idea Jericho faced decimation not just once, but several times, including during the era that scholars believe the Bible refers to, at least, in general. Moreover, why kill all the animals, as well?

If not God, then who did want this? Did extraterrestrials order this mass murder of thousands, along with all their livestock and various animals? If so, why? One supposes that one possible answer would be to wipe out some possible type of pestilence that might have existed in the city. This might not cause immediate symptoms, but might have longer-term repercussions for people. Perhaps animals housed in the city carried the disease, as well, and this might have been the reason for such a wholesale extermination.

When we think how long HIV (AIDS) can take to appear in some infected victims, sometimes years to a decade or even longer to manifest, this is hardly a farfetched idea. Moreover, some diseases, even of today, affect both animals and humans, as with the Bird Flu. Subsequently, the idea of their being a long-term pestilence developing in the city isn't a farfetched one.

Therefore, what was still a massacre, although a terrible one might have been necessary to halt the advance and spread of such a type of disease, one that might have eventually infected all of humanity? Of course, we wouldn't know about such an illness now, because it might well be extinct, made so by just this sort of appalling cleansing of the population.

Nonetheless, we still have the question of why alien beings might care about this matter one way or another, even if so. Why would they order the mass movement of Jews from Egypt in the first place to an area that later would become the modern region known as Israel?

Why all the stipulations as to how to go about it and then periodic direct interventions by such beings from another world, for if it was not God who caused the plagues of Egypt, then "they" must have been instrumental somehow in their spread, instead?

Again, one has to ask why they would go through such massive effort, aid those people with "miracles," and then have them wipe out a native people, including their animals, to occupy a new region. Such beings had to have had a purpose, some sort of long-range goal in order to go through such great efforts over so long a period.

Likewise, that purpose had to include a reasonably intimate knowledge of the longstanding outcomes of the actions they were taking, the consequences of their repeated interventions. The results of their actions, as they must have known, would echo not just for decades and centuries, but perhaps for millennia to come, and just as they seem to have actually done.

To have a purpose in doing this at all, such extraterrestrials would necessarily have to know the outcome of such actions, or at least, have a good idea of the repercussions of doing such things. Otherwise, why go through what must have been a truly major effort on their part?

In short, could whoever had structured this whole series of events culminating in the wanton laying waste of a country's inhabitants, cities, people and animals, not have had the ability to time travel, or at least to see the consequences or outcome of their actions far into the future? It seems unlikely they could not have had such abilities under the circumstances, or how else could they determine the long-term consequences of their actions, would know how they would work out the way they wanted them to?

Similarly, we see repeatedly such interventions of this sort related to us throughout the Old Testament. Again, who was doing all this intervening if we are discounting God as the culprit? To put it down to aliens or extraterrestrials doing this is one answer. However, I feel this solution is an insufficient one.

These interventions were too large scale to be arbitrary interventions. There has to have been some sort of object or goal. To have such a goal, again, these beings had to be able somehow to predict, and with marvelous accuracy, what the outcomes of such interventions would be over the long haul.

So either they had marvelously predictive computers, and that is possible, or some other explanation must be found. Remember that according to the Old Testament:

1. The future-altering events were not only numerous during this time period, but

2. Occurred at seemingly very specific moments in history, at various nexus points in our timeline when things could have gone very differently otherwise, and

3. The consequences of such interventions caused extremely long-term "ripple effects" down through time, throughout our history from that point forward, and to the very present.

For example, the Middle East as we know it today would have been utterly different if the Israelites had not made their exodus from Egypt. There would have been no modern state of Israel in all likelihood. There may not even have been a continuation of the Jewish people as a separate and distinct race, culture, and religious group. They could well have been absorbed into the Egyptian culture over the ensuing millennia to such an extent they wouldn't be an individual race or creed today at all, but instead have gradually melted away into the dominate civilization of the times.

Only by having left Egypt and then later becoming the Kingdoms of Judah and Israel, did the Jewish culture and civilization manage to remain intact and distinctive for as long as it did and during very troubled times. The Jewish culture survived where it otherwise very well might have been absorbed. There is more.

All scholars of religion acknowledge Judaism as the parent of both the Islamic and the Christian religions and all their various offshoots. Therefore, by interfering in history in this way at this particular time, "whoever" did this would have wrought inconceivable changes, but ones, since they are now part of our history, hardly even question.

Ask yourself this; if the Jewish people hadn't left Egypt and then founded their own nation, would the world be anything like it is today or would it be utterly different? If the answer is no, that it would not be the same at all, that it would be completely different, then we have established that the event of the Jews leaving Egypt and taking the area known as Israel today was a nexus point, a crisis (turning) point in human history. Additionally, it was a monumental one.

Moreover, it seems "someone" was instrumental in causing these events; some outside force induced these changes. Again, the idea aliens were responsible for this is not necessarily wrong in my opinion, but if so, they had to have a very intimate knowledge of how these changes would change the future world of humanity. Even we don't have that capability yet and we are human!

The extraterrestrials would also have to have a major reason for going through so much effort to cause these changes, some overriding goal. Just what goal would aliens have for doing this? Why would they care about future human events one way or the other?

Where time travelers might well have some knowledge, know what it would take to alter the timeline the way they wanted, and had the power to do it, I am not at all sure extraterrestrials would have all this knowledge. They might have the capability of such interference, by again, why would they bother? How would they know what the outcomes of such interference would be?

Furthermore, what purpose would they have in altering our future timeline? Again, whoever did this not only went to great effort, made great changes, seemed to be able to predict the results of those changes, but also they must have had a good reason for wanting to do all this.

Repeatedly, as mentioned above, there are examples of these godlike or otherworldly interventions in the affairs of men. Moreover, as also mentioned above, the results didn't just affect the Jewish people, but all peoples around them in the end and as a direct consequence. Nor do we just have to rely on the Old Testament to see this sort of major interference in our history.

**Alexander The Great**. No less a person than Alexander the Great had his conquering of the known world interfered with by "someone." As mentioned in my sister book, *Time Travel: 35 Cases of Time Travel Intrusion* (Please see a link under *"References"*), the year was 329 BCE. The place was along the banks of the Indus River, India. Alexander had camped his army there prior to making the crossing and invasion. However, at this point, flying "silver shields" buzzed them from the sky, frightening the soldiers and causing the war elephants to go berserk.

The action was clearly intimidating and deliberately meant to be, it seems. In short, it seemed quite purposeful and purposely disruptive in the description given. The result was Alexander's army balked at crossing the river. They felt the "flying shields" were an ill omen of major proportions.

Consummate general that Alexander was, he did manage to restore order and rallied the troops. Ultimately, they did make the river crossing. However, in short order, so mutinous had his men become, so desirous were they of going home, so bad was their morale by this point that Alexander, at long last, gave into their wishes. He stopped his eastern expansion of his empire. He headed back toward the west.

This was another of those crucial nexus points. Had Alexander not had this "flying shield" incident, he would undoubtedly have continued eastward, conquered all of India and perhaps more regions beyond. He did not. His conquest toward the east stopped there.

The interference of the "flying shields" seems to have been pivotal in his decision not to do this. All history would have been different if he'd continued with his original plans. He might not have made his rendezvous with death so early in his life, but lived a longer one, instead. His favorite general and companion, Hephaestus, might not have died either, when he did.

The Alexandrian empire might have thus lasted far longer than it did, as well. Instead of just creating a "Panhellenic" culture around the entire region of Europe and Asia, we might have had a centuries-lasting Alexandrian Empire remaining intake, instead of having it collapse upon his death and then immediately carved up into independent regions with various people ruling each portion, such as the Ptolemy Dynasty in Egypt.

Would this have made major changes in our history? Oh, yes! Additionally, they would have been very big ones, huge in fact. The Roman Empire might never have existed or if it had, not have been able to defend itself against such a mighty Alexandrian Empire. This would mean that Western Europe, which received much of its modern day inheritance from the Romans, such as law, architecture, art, culture, etc., might never have occurred. Instead, there might have been a much stronger eastern influence than there was otherwise. Our culture today would have been very different, accordingly.

Moreover, Alexander's own historian related these incidents. He gave these accounts to us. Nor was this the end of the otherworldly interference according to him. A number of years later, Alexander laid siege to the famous city of Tyre, the main city of the Phoenicians of the time. It was at this point that multiple witnesses on both sides of the battle, according to the same historian, say something truly inexplicable occurred. They report something appeared in the skies, a flying shield again, or something very like it, apparently. A beam of light or fire shot from the craft and struck one of the walls of the city. The wall buckled and fell, allowing Alexander and his men to invaded Tyre.

Again, history was changed and dramatically so. We do know that Alexander did conquer Tyre. We also know that at the time, the city was a well-defended and extremely well-fortified (walled) metropolis. Defeating Tyre gave Alexander unchallenged rule over the entire region. His reign there was unchallenged by anyone as a result, since nobody remained whom he hadn't conquered already.

Now, what do we make of all this? If the historian and witnesses spoke the truth, then again, "someone" interfered with human events in a very big way, and not just once, but twice. The first time, it seems to have been to halt the advance of Alexander's empire any farther to the east, as if they did not want this for some reason.

The second time, it seems to have been in his aid of conquering the city of Tyre and securing his hold in the west. This, "they" seemed to want.

Of course, questions arise. Would Alexander have failed to win the siege without such interference of these "others?" Did "they" somehow know this and so stepped in to alter events yet again? Alexander has gone down in history as unconquerable. If he had failed to achieve his goal with Tyre, this wouldn't have been so. Today, we might not even know him as "Alexander the Great." His place in history thus might have been much less, smaller in scale, scope, and nature. The great Panhellenic culture for which he was responsible might never have happened.

Furthermore, following historical events would again have been very different. Twice, there was outside interference, it seems, with regard to Alexander, and twice these occurred at apparent nexus points in human history, thus vastly changing the course of the future as a result.

Are we to think these are just meddling extraterrestrials interfering for no apparent reason? This would seem unlikely.

Alternatively, whether time-traveling extraterrestrials or our own time-traveling descendants, were they the ones who had intimate knowledge of the course of future events and so deliberately interfered to alter them for some purpose, some preferred outcome?

Why else would these intrusions have occurred when they did, when they had the most power to alter and reshape the course of things to come? Alien, human, or post-human—it seems someone was meddling with our timeline. They must had had reasons of their own, perhaps specific outcomes they desired as a reason to do this. Otherwise, why these precise types of intrusions?

There are more such instances of this sort of intrusion and alteration of the course of human events, many in fact. Again, there simply isn't room here in this book for all of them. However, what are we to make of this other than:

1. Someone was acting deliberately by interfering,

2. They must have had a reason and that reason obviously was to alter the outcome of events, otherwise they just make no sense as random intrusions for no good reason,

3. The outcome of events was altered deliberately to achieve some desired goal, and

4. "They" had to know this in advance, have knowledge of how things would go if they hadn't interfered at such critical junctures in our history. In short, they were deliberately rewriting our history, our timeline, and for reasons of their own.

Now with regard to these ancient events, I have deliberately picked those that took place in recorded history. Did interference occur before we started writing down our past? Quite possibly, but it is harder to know with any certainty if this was actually so. Yet, given the ongoing nature of such interference in our timeline, one might well assume it didn't just start when we began the recording of such events. That would seem rather arbitrary and even naïve on our part to think such a thing…

Nor did it stop with intrusions into our more ancient past. It would seem there might well have been such interferences on an ongoing basis. *In Mysteries of Time Travel: 35 Cases of Time Travel Intrusion,* I go into more depth on this subject, with regard to the history of Europe and Asia, as well as the United States. (Again, please see *"References"* at the end of this book for a link.) Here, I only touch on the subject because of space limitations, and the fact this subject constitutes only one aspect of time travel and time travelers.

However, here's a short list of some other possible time travel intrusions:

**China Interfered with by "Divine Wind."** China for centuries wanted to seize control of Japan. Finally, they tried to do this. The Mongol Emperor, Kublai Khan, send a large fleet to invade Japan. He tried to do this in 1274 CE.

The attempt failed. A great wind and resulting storm, known now by the Japanese as the Kamikaze, or "Divine Wind," interfered with the emperor's plans. His fleet sank and his soldiers, for the most part, drowned. What few men who did survive and make it to the Japanese Islands were summarily executed, it seems.

The Japanese hailed the Kamikaze, or "Divine Wind" as just that, a wind that was divine, one sent by the gods to save them from an impossibly large invasion force, one they had no hope of repelling otherwise.

The Japanese might have been guilty of a certain hubris, since storms and "great winds" do happen. Therefore, this event, although a crucial pivotal point in history, another one of those critical nexus points, could have been just a terrible coincidence for the Chinese and their fleet.

However, Kublai Khan was not one to give up so easily. He mounted yet another invasion force some seven years later in 1281 CE. This one had over 140,000 troops involved in the attack force. It seems the Mongolian Emperor was taking no chances with this second attempt. He wanted victory!

He didn't get it. Yet another "Divine Wind" or Kamikaze struck his fleet and destroyed it and most of his men…again! This was the emperor's and China's final attempt to take Japan. They gave it up as a lost cause. Even they felt the gods were against them in the endeavor, and one can easily see why, because two such ill-fated attempts, both thwarted by great winds/storms, couldn't have been just coincidence. Or could it? Not only did this happen twice, which does seem incredibly unlucky for the Chinese (although lucky, perhaps, for the Japanese of the times), but each time the destruction of the forces of China were at an incredible level. The storms didn't just reduce the size of the Emperor's military expeditions, but utterly wiped them out! If "someone" was behind these divine winds, they didn't take any chances with the outcomes, it seems.

Again, this was a crucial turning point in history. If either attempt had succeeded, the future of the world, including Japan's later intimate involvement in two world wars, most likely would not have occurred. History, our timeline, would have been not just different, but dramatically so!

So did someone or something instigate these "divine winds" somehow? Even we are now talking about interfering weather. We have already done this by accident without even trying, as with global warming, so the idea is hardly beyond consideration.

In any case, the Japanese were so impressed with the wind, they gave it the name, "Kamikaze," the Divine Wind," and that name would stick for centuries to come, and also be integral in how they behaved in future times. A whole cultural mythos would arise based on the idea of the Kamikaze. There are other famous cases of divine winds.

**Spanish Attempts To Invade England Stopped By a Divine Storm.** Many of us, especially those who are history buffs, have heard of the defeat of the great Spanish Armada in its attempt to invade England in 1588 CE. A fleet of some 130 or so ships and a force of some 60,000 soldiers ended this endeavor in tragedy when a great storm and wind destroyed the fleet.

This was referred to by many historians as a very "sudden storm." So happy was Queen Elizabeth I of the times about this outcome that she and her court officially used the phrase, *"Wind of God."* Moreover, she had *"God Blew And They Were Scattered"* engraved on memorial medallions she had struck especially for the occasion. Again, was this a divine wind, or a Kamikaze, as the Japanese called it?

Moreover, this was an incredible nexus point in history, as well. If Spain had successfully invaded, the country, then they would have forced England to return to Catholicism. Since the middle class and free enterprise went hand-in-hand, the forcing of most of Western Europe back to the Church wits its rigid class structure might well have delayed the Industrial Revolution for a long time to come. That is, even if it ever occurred there with the explosive and expansive force it did (first happening in England.)

**America's Divine Wind and Great Storm.** Divine winds seem almost habitual in history at times. For instance, in the War of 1812, the British landed on the eastern coast of the United States and marched on Washington D.C. The nation's capital hurriedly evacuated just ahead of the oncoming troops.

As the triumphant English marched their troops down the main boulevard of Washington, setting fire to everything in sight as they went, including the White House, there was no doubt they had won the day by anyone witnessing this catastrophe. That is, until "as if out of nowhere" a "hurricane" struck the area in a highly localized way. Even a tornado went right down the main street, decimating the British forces, and thus causing them to scatter and retreat.

Later, this "hurricane," again so localized as only seeming to have really affected the poor British and nobody else, was officially "The Storm of Providence." This was because it was so "providential" (meaning "from God") as to save our nation's capital and so keep it under American control.

Again, if the British had burned the place to the ground, the effect on American morale would have been devastating. Nor is it likely the English forces would stop there, but rather they would continue.

This didn't happen. Instead, it seems the "Storm of Providence" inspired Americans to fight all the harder, since "God was on our side," or so they, at least, felt.

**Chapter Conclusion**: There is much more in this vein of such strange interference in our history. Of course, since it is now a part of history, we tend to think it "has" to be a normal part of it.

Yet, repeatedly we see that it was not normal, but extraordinary, so much so that the peoples of the times involved, often both sides in the events, saw these winds and their attendant storms as divine intervention and "providential." Some struck coins or cast medallions, and official titles labeled the storms as divine in nature.

Therefore, even by the people involved at the time, these were not ordinary events. Moreover, such winds certainly were not typical with regard to those who experienced them. The storms, themselves, were unusual in their ferocity, and not just their perfect timing.

Moreover, they all occurred at incredibly critical moments in history, during events that would have otherwise changed our timeline in so great a manner as to make our world of today virtually nonexistent, no doubt! So were these just accidental occurrences all happening at such critical times, and all involving providential or divine winds?

Alternatively, were they the result of direct interference by someone, a "someone" who wanted to alter the probable course of events differently from their otherwise predicted outcomes?

Even if we can't quite bring ourselves to believe such a thing is possible, one thing is clear. The people involved consistently and always felt that someone was interfering in their affairs, whether God, gods, or some "divine" force, providential or otherwise.

People around the planet, including those of the United States, felt that there was such interference. Perhaps, they are more right than they knew, but also partly wrong. For the divine force may have not been so divine in nature, but just the product of highly advanced beings from a future time interfering in ours.

Once more, for a much more in-depth look at these and other events, including the terrible flood in Lynmouth, Devon, England, in 1952, please see the link to *Mysteries of Time Travel: 35 Cases of Time Travel Intrusion* under the "*References*" section at the end of this book. The idea of time travelers using weather interference to change the course of events is a theory I've developed. It is a controversial one, of course, but again, after looking at the evidence, it is up to readers to decide for themselves.

# CHAPTER 9
# People Disappearing Into Other Timelines?

*"It's hard to know which stars in the sky will turn into black holes. And which ones will open up worm holes into entire new universes."*

— James Altucher

Not only do we have people in our timeline who claim to have been living other lives in some parallel reality subtly different from ours, but we also have people who have apparently disappeared from our timeline into another, as well. This would seem to be a necessary thing. After all, if we can accept the idea that people are "popping" into our reality, we would also then expect the phenomenon would work in the reverse, as well, with people popping out of our reality into another one at different times and locations.

This does seem to happen. Repeatedly, we have had reports of the mysterious disappearances of individuals, groups of people, and even ships, planes, vehicles, and sometimes even the populations of entire villages. (For more on this, please see, *Deadly UFOS And The Disappeared* link under *"References"* at the end of this book.)

Therefore, the fluidity of being able to move from one parallel time stream to another seems to work in both directions. If this is sort of thing is truly so, if we can find evidence for this, then our reality is far from being as fixed as we might think it is.

First, this idea of people transiting to other realities should not be so surprising to us. Quantum Theory states quite clearly, as we shall see in another chapter, that on the microscopic level, the level of subatomic particles that make up atoms, which in turn make up us and everything else in our world, reality is far less fixed. In fact, reality as we think of it, doesn't really exist at all some would say. Many quantum scientists also say the same thing about time on such a subatomic level.

Therefore, it is only on the macroscopic level, the larger level of existence that we all live in, which includes not only us, but all other physical objects of size in our universe, such as cars, boats, trees, oceans, mountains, stars, planets, snails and all, that things seem solid and "real."

Not so, according to some recent and hard evidence that scientists have discovered, but again, we will discuss this in another chapter later on. For now, let's concentrate on the world, as we know it, and the strange things that have taken place in it over the last centuries, at least according to many witnesses of various backgrounds.

These witnesses include friends of the victims, relatives, legal authorities such as the police, and others who were complete strangers, who had no reason to lie, and every reason to be objective about what they saw. In addition, what they saw often was very strange, indeed, to the point of being virtually inexplicable, as with the following case:

**The Disappearing Professor.** First reported in Venezuela in the *El Tiempo* newspaper, is the story of a man who simply vanished from this world. One day, at the University of Andes, Merida, Venezuela, a long-time and popular professor, walked to his car.

This was in front of many witnesses, both students, as well as others. This is clearly stated in the newspaper account, which even goes so far as to say that some of the witnesses even hailed him as he walked by them, so there was no doubt this actually happened, as far as they were all concerned.

The professor climbed into his vehicle, closed the door, but did not leave the parking lot. In fact, the car didn't move at all, but just remained parked where it was. At first, those nearby were unconcerned and thought perhaps he was just resting, eating his lunch, or something of such a nature.

As time passed, however, curiosity grew. Finally, several people approached the car. They looked inside of the vehicle. To their amazement, the students found the thing was empty.

Their friendly teacher had disappeared. No sign of him was to be found and there was no way he could have left the car without them having seen him do so, since the car had been in plain sight, being parked as it was out in the open in the lot all the time, and it having been broad daylight when the event occurred.

The man was gone. He was never to return. This was the final disposition of the case and despite long-term efforts by police and detectives to locate the professor, alive or dead. The original reporter of this for *El Tiempo*, Senor Segundo Peña, continued to follow up on the case, despite this disposition, including having interviews with the local constabulary, etc., but all to no avail. Nobody saw the professor again, not ever. At least, nobody saw him again in this reality...

Just what had happened to the professor? Well, obviously it is a matter of conjecture, since we can't know for sure. Nevertheless, we have certain facts. Many clearly saw him cross a parking lot in broad daylight and then get into his car. Although people stayed in the area continuously and had the car easily in their sight the whole time, they never saw his car leave, or him get out of it. Yet, he somehow vanished forever.

Police, detectives, and reporters could never discover what happened to the man after that. There was no trace of him from that point forward, not there, or anywhere else, they could ascertain. He was just…gone. These, too, are also the simple facts.

In addition, given these facts, it definitely would seem something of an extraordinary nature happened to the man. Did he get into his car and drive off, but this time it was in a parallel universe in an otherwise identical car? Did he go on with his life as if nothing had ever happened, except just not in this universe? Did he "fall" through a hole in time and space as so many others of those who have vanished are said to have, and so ended up in some alien dimension? No one knows for sure. The only thing that we know is he disappeared within plain sight of multiple witnesses under excellent viewing conditions.

In this case, the man seems to have disappeared altogether from this reality into another one. However, just where did he go? What was this other reality like? Again, we may never know. However, it could well be a different timeline, one very similar to our own, but just enough different to cause him to vanish here for good when he entered it.

**People Disappear All The Time And Forever.** People vanish in their thousands every year. By one estimate, as many as 900,000 or more persons disappear in the United States alone on an annual basis (figure appears to have even risen above that amount in recent years) and about five percent of these we never seen again. **An important note here**: this is the remaining figure after subtracting for those who were kidnapped, murdered, or just didn't want to be found. After deducting all that, there is still that five percent amount we cannot account for in any way.

Incredibly, that five percent still comes to about 45,000 people a year! Again, that's only in the United States, and these same percentages seem to hold true around the world. In some places, the disappearance rate is even much higher, but wars and military conflicts are probably the culprit in such particularly high rates of disappearance, since these larger figures come from such war-torn locations. However, remember, even if only the five percent as we have here in the United States never are seen again, then we are still talking about thousands upon tens of thousands of people disappearing each year...and forever.

So huge are these numbers that many authors have written books on the subject, including the *Missing* book series by David Paulides, as just one example. Therefore, the question has to be raised, in these modern times with so much data tracking, with so many of us now with cellphones, tablets, and such with location software and hardware built into them, how can so many people still vanish and so utterly without a trace? Moreover, how can they disappear forever?

There is a variety of possibilities, and many people feel there are probably different answers, such as Mr. Paulides. However, the truth is that there may be more than one answer. In addition, one of these answers could well be that people simply just "pop" out of this reality into another one. Again, there are those who claim to have done just that in reverse, and have come here from "somewhere else." Logic would seem to indicate if this is so, than the reverse must be true, as well.

**Conclusion:** The example of the disappearing professor is just one of hundreds of well-documented disappearances. There are many, many others! In the most severe cases, the persons vanish without a trace, often from plain sight, and never seen again. The possibilities of how this can be are few, as with a man who fell forward in a road, while he was running, but followed close behind by friends in a pony cart. He fell and then simply disappeared right in plain sight of them. Again, and again this happens.

So where are all these people going? If they are gone for good from our realm, then they must have gone somewhere else. To where is the question. Do they all go to the same place, or different places? Is someone or something abducting them somehow, or are these just "natural" accidents?

One way of answering these questions is to consider those who say they did the same thing, but came here from elsewhere to here. Do we have such people? Yes, we have a few. Now, in the next chapter, we will look at some of these instances.

# CHAPTER 10
# Alternate Timeline Memories?

*"... [L]et me tell you a secret: Some of the remarkable people you meet in life are time travelers. A few of these people know it; the others time travel without realizing it, but they do it just the same...."*

—Fred Alan Wolf, *The Yoga of Time Travel*

Alternate timeline memories are a strange phenomenon, as we shall see later on with something known as the Mandela Effect. Some alternate memories are so bizarre that in many cases, it is very hard to explain them by any normal means. Numerous individuals report strange alternate memories, ones they insist are real, and in some cases, even have some physical evidence to support their contentions.

Many of these people have also gone to extraordinary lengths and expense to try to resolve their predicament, even to the point of doubting their own sanity. In order to resolve the issues of such odd memories, they have attended family doctors for consultations, done the same when they visited psychiatrists.

Some even resorted to hiring private detectives and much more in some instances. They did all this just to try to prove their claims are valid or that they are, as individuals, suffering from some sort of mental break. This may seem like an odd thing for them to want to prove, that they have had a mental breakdown, but for many of these people, even this outcome is preferable to what they think has really happened to them, which is frightening in the extreme.

MS Lerina Garcia is an example. She tried all these things as we will shall shortly see, and found no resolution to her problems. She is convinced she remembers a past differently from the one she now has. What's worse is she lost loved ones, people she remembers loving and cherishing, sometimes for years, and persons who mattered to her very much. Now, as she claims, they vanished from her life, literally as if they never existed, except in her memory alone, but nobody else's.

Furthermore, these alternate timeline memories, such as MS Garcia has, aren't just restricted to the few. Tens of thousands of people remember something differently from how it actually happened. Can people retain memories of another life, an alternate, but still one with very similar aspects in many respects to their current one?

Yes, it seems they can. However, nobody seems to really be able to account for this weird phenomenon, other than to simply say that thousands have remembered something wrongly and sometimes it seems…very wrongly, at least, compared to their current reality.

In any case, alternate timeline memories, that is, remembering things from the past differently than they happened in this timeline is a real occurrence. For some, it isn't just the timeline of their memories that altered, but their current lives, as well, as with Lerina Garcia.

Memories of a current lover, one's child, or a friend can stay, while again, the persons themselves vanished from the victim's life. Imagine waking up one morning and having something like this happen to you. It has for other people, such as Lerina:

**The Mysterious Case of Lerina García.** Here is an odd case, a very odd case, indeed, but it seems one well documented, as far as the basic facts go. This story is here as a representative of many such types of cases. Although any particular account might have "holes" in it, again, there are so many of them, as to warrant their addition here as a form of contributing evidence, at the very least. After all, if enough people witness something strange, perhaps there is something strange going on?

The story of Lerina Garcia, a well-educated woman, begins when she awoke one day to an odd set of circumstances. Her life seemed fundamentally different but only in certain ways and this confused her. Small things and some big things had abruptly changed. The apartment was the same, but some small aspects of the furnishings were different. For example, the sheets on her bed were strange to her, unfamiliar, although the bed seemed the same otherwise.

The worrisome part of all this for Lerina was she didn't have amnesia. Such a thing would have been a simple enough explanation. It would have been one with which she could more easily have dealt, but no, she remembered her past and her life very well. She just remembered it as being different from the life and history she was now suddenly experiencing.

For her, it was as if she had landed in another world, and had assumed someone else's identity. This other "someone" seemed to have been very much like herself in most respects, but also to have been different in others. Lerina was at a loss as to explain why this was so.

So was everyone else she knew, or thought she knew…As examples of these changes, for instance, although her automobile was the same, and so was the company she worked for and the location of it, the department she had worked in no longer was hers. They insisted she worked over in another section of the building entirely and in an entirely different department.

Wondering what was wrong with her, Lerina went to her physician, and had a drug and alcohol test taken. The results were negative. Lerina had no sign of drugs in here, in any way. Neither was she in any way under the influence of alcohol.

As time passed, more oddities surfaced and some of these were big ones! Her relationships, for example, had altered. This even included more than one person utterly disappearing from her life. She remembered having had a relationship with a man for seven and a half years and then had broken it off with him. She had then started on another romance with a man by the name of Augustin. Together for four months, Lerina knew his full name, of course, as well as his address. She also knew his place of employment, a boy he had fathered from a prior relationship, and where the man was taking classes. She remembered many details about him.

However, now in this new world, meaning our world, Lerina could find no trace of him. It was as if he had never existed at all, but she remembered him very well, in detail, both him, and their relationship.

Desperate now, she even hired a detective. He could find no evidence of her lover ever having existed. Nor could she find any trace of his son. He and his family had simply vanished from existence, as if they never had been.

Instead, she discovered she was still in the prior relationship of the man she had been with for over seven years earlier. Apparently, their intimate association had never ended in our timeline.

Lerina even went to a psychiatrist of her own volition. The doctor, who although feeling she was mentally competent, felt she must be suffering from stress-related hallucinations of some sort. Yet, those hallucinations were incredibly specific, and totally unlike normal hallucinations.

For example, her sister, who she remembered as having had a shoulder surgery performed on her just months before, now had no recollection of any such surgery ever having taken place. The rest of the family was the same way in this, with no memory of anything like a surgery having occurred.

To this day, Lerina swears all this is true. She is obviously flummoxed by the changes in her life, in her past, and she simply can't account for any of it, except, perhaps to think she had switched over somehow to a parallel universe that was much the same, but different in some minor and major aspects. She is desperate to find out exactly what has happened to her, and on the Internet, she posted this plea in 2008:

*"Please, if someone has had a similar experience, please contact me to see what may have happened.*

*"I cannot find any pathology that matches my experience. For five months I've been reading all of the theories I've come across and am convinced that it has been a jump between planes or something, a decision or action taken that has caused things to change...Has anyone had a similar experience? Pranksters and people with a grasp on 'the truth' can refrain from commenting. This is very serious to me..."*

The plea is included here (not in its entirety); just in case anyone who reads this book can help Lerina in any way in this matter.

This does sound very much like a case of someone having jumped from one reality to an alternate one and then being stuck there (here?). However, what if her memories actually fit the category of so-called "false memories" in the special sense, meaning, and as will be shown later in the chapter on the "Mandela Effect," that Lerina remembers a different timeline? Could this be the case instead of her coming from an alternate universe? Did our timeline change and Lerina remembers it as it was, rather than as it is now, and before some time traveler's intervention changed it, while almost all of the rest of us have forgotten?

As we can see, there is more than one possible explanation for what has happened to MS Garcia. Regardless of the explanation, for Lerina, this must be a frustrating and tragic situation. Not only is she afraid she might be mentally unbalanced, but for her, she has seen a love of her life wiped out as if he had never existed at all. It's one thing to have loved and lost, but another matter entirely for everyone to insist the person you loved never existed at all, that the love she knew to be real, never even having happened.

Moreover, there is another aspect to this story. If Lerina Garcia did arrive here from an alternate reality, *what then happened to the original Lerina that was already here?* Did they exchange places? Did the original Lerina of this reality simply cease to be? Again, the possibilities are frightening.

Nor is MS Lerina Garcia alone in this matter, as we mentioned. She is just one representative case. There are others. We will include one more as a further and rather famous example:

**The Man From Taured.** This is a popular story that has circulated on the Internet for years. Repeatedly, different people relate the tale and several books and periodicals discuss it.

Supposedly, a man from a nonexistent country showed up in Tokyo in or around 1954, and with what appeared to be a valid passport, stamped and from a country in Europe called Taured. However, no such country ever existed. He also had other documentation that was equally inexplicable, such as a checkbook, complete with checks from a nonexistent bank.

Finally, not knowing what else to do, and not knowing how to deport him back to a nonexistent place, the Japanese authorities put him under house arrest in a hotel room. They ordered him not to leave. However, when they went back, he and his things had vanished. Nobody saw him again.

Is this story true? Well, although it has survived for a long duration, little evidence for it is available one way or the other. My personal feeling is the tale might well be fiction. However, evidence either for or against this idea is almost utterly lacking. Apparently, several works, though, including, but not limited to *Into Thin Air: People Who Disappear* by Paul Begg, as well as in *Strange But True: Mysterious and Bizarre People*, by author Thomas Slemen, as well as others do reference the story.

This last story has an interesting side note, which further deepens the mystery. *Strange But True: Mysterious And Bizarre People* is on **Google Books**. Yet, according to "Lucia" at one website (please see *"References"*), she claims a portion of the book is not there, is in fact missing. This includes the references section of that book. Therefore, any such references for the *Man From Taured* couldn't be found by her.

If some of the book is missing there, why is it missing? It's a good question, but one seemingly without an answer, apparently, at least for the present. Why are newspaper articles on the matter also impossible to find? Did those never exist, despite supposedly having reported on the event, because the story is an old urban myth?

Alternatively, have any such references been purposely deleted by someone? Is it possible there is a conspiracy to wipe out any evidence of this event actually having happened, although it might have? The answers, of course, are is that nobody currently knows. Yet, the fact of the missing portion of the book is a little strange, especially since the missing section also included the very necessary references section for the Taured case. Conspiracy theorists might make much of this point...

# CHAPTER 11
# The Mandela Effect

*"According to 'M' theory, ours is not the only universe. Instead, 'M' theory predicts that a great many universes were created out of nothing."*

— Stephen Hawking

In the last chapter, we have discussed the idea of people who remember a different life other than the one they have sometimes awakened to, as in the case of Lerina Garcia. We have also discussed people seeing and/or interacting with what appears to have been events and people from the past, and sometimes even the future.

There is another type of time phenomenon, as well, and one so well recognized, it has earned the name, the "Mandela Effect." Mandela is in reference to Nelson Mandela, the African hero of the Apartheid era of South Africa, as well as later becoming that country's president. His was a brave and illustrious career. However, here we are not talking about the man himself, or his deeds, but oddly enough, about the memories others have of him.

The term, Mandela Effect was first used by MS Fiona Broome to describe a strange phenomenon. Specifically, it concerned the bizarre memory of many people that Nelson Mandela, while still a prisoner of the Apartheid regime in South Africa, passed away.

He did so while still imprisoned. This, many people remember as having occurred in the late 1980's.

Now, the number of people we're talking about here is not a paltry figure, but a lot! In addition, this phenomenon of them remembering Nelson Mandela as having expired several decades ago is a worldwide one. For many, the man never lived to see his freedom. Yet he did and he went on to become president, no less. Despite this, this weird memory of many persists, even so.

These people, to put it concisely, remember two different versions of the death of Nelson Mandela, one from decades ago, and one much more recently. Both sets of memories exist in their minds at the same time! How can this be? Were they in error? Did they just get it "wrong?"

At first glance, one would think so, that being the obvious and easiest answer, but the sheer numbers of people who "remember" his death in the 1980's is truly staggering. As one person put it, it is an "absurd" number of people who remember his death this way. Yet, these same people are also fully aware he died much later, and only after the time he was no longer the president. This is a truly eerie set of circumstances, the idea that so many people could have two diametrically opposed sets of memories about something like this.

Neither does the phenomenon stop with Nelson Mandela with the date and circumstances of his death. There are numerous other examples. For instance, many thousands of people while still students in school, insist they were taught that New Zealand was in a much different location on the map than it really is. The same holds true for the island of Sri Lanka off the eastern coast of India.

This last one has particular relevance for me, because I was a strong student of geography, even when very young. Just for fun, while others doodled away in class while listening to a teacher drone on, I would draw the maps of the world on sheets of paper. I always put Sri Lanka in the wrong spot, apparently, *and exactly where many others thought it was supposed to be, as well!*

Why Sri Lanka, but no other place? Why would my memory of the location of that island be so wrong when all the other places I remember on maps were right? Moreover, it seems I wasn't alone in this "error," since it was a major example of the Mandela Effect. Therefore, it seems I've been a personal victim of this effect, as well, whatever it is...

The thing here is people can get the locations of islands on maps wrong. Nobody is infallible, of course. However, the strange thing here is that so many persons get the same thing wrong, and only that one thing *and in the same way!* Even more telling is that they remember and so reposition the island in the *same wrong place!* How do we account for this peculiar fact?

Were we all just poor geography students? It's certainly possible, but I assure you that in this particular instance, I was not. I loved geography and history to the point where I read my textbooks through entirely in the first week that I received them. I had a truly avid interest in these subjects to the point, again, I drew world maps as a form of doodling, repeatedly, hundreds of times when bored and listening to my teachers going on about something far less interesting (in my opinion).

Always, I put the island in the wrong place, and in the same wrong place that many others did! Again, if this is just a result of bad geography lessons, or a disinclination to pay attention, why this island and why did we keep placing it in the same wrong location? This is a massive and odd set of coincidences, at the very least…

Moreover, for those who still insist on claiming all of us were just bad geography students; do remember that these people didn't make the same mistake with countless other islands and countries. They got those facts right. Furthermore, anyone who wishes to see my grades for geography in Junior High, High School, and University are welcome to, if only to help prove my point.

There are more such examples. As another illustration, many remember the *"Berenstein Bears."* These were a series of children's book by authors Jan and Stan Berenstain. In reality (apparently), the title of the series is the **Berenstain Bears**, with "Berenstain" spelled with an "a" and not an "e."

This may seem a trivial example, but not so! So many insist they remember the title with the "e" in it rather than the "a" that there is even a conspiracy theory surrounding the subject. In other words, this isn't just a few people. Rather, many remember the name spelled differently than it now is. Did they all just get that wrong, too, or is this a symptom of something else. Remember, these people are so adamant on this subject, they feel there is a conspiracy going on about it. That's adamant!

There are more examples yet, numerous ones, in fact. As just a couple more instances, there is the case of the "missing portrait of Henry VIII." Large numbers of people swear they had seen at some point in their life a copy of the portrait of King Henry VIII of England eating a turkey leg.

Others argue this was a leg of mutton, or perhaps some other bird, such as a swan or goose, but they don't argue the fact they saw such a picture.

However, *there is no such portrait* as far as the experts are concerned and there never was one! So how do we account for so many people remembering this picture that never existed? Again, these are many people, all of whom agree on the same particular issue, this time about Henry VIII and his turkey leg. Why do so many people insist up on this portrait as having been real?

Then there is also the matter of the color, chartreuse, as well. Wikipedia defines Chartreuse as being:

*"...a color halfway between yellow and green that was named because of its resemblance to the green color of one of the French liqueurs called green chartreuse..."*

Yet, many people, in their thousands, either remember chartreuse as being a shade of red, magenta or sometimes referred to as "maroonish" in color. That's very different from yellow-green. Besides, *they all remember it as being the same alternate color*, rather than various and different ones that they might have otherwise remembered. Again, not only did they all get chartreuse wrong, but also *they all got it wrong in the exact same way!*

As an intriguing side note, I spoke of this Mandela Effect to Randy Allan Cloney II, a friend of mine. I mentioned I had been a "victim" of it with regard to remembering Sri Lanka as being in the wrong place like so many others. I also mentioned the memory some have of Nelson Mandela having died not just a few years ago, but a couple of decades, ago, instead.

Then, just out of curiosity, I asked him what color "chartreuse" was. His answer? He said it was a "deep, very, dark red, like that of some types of flower petals!" Randy, it seems, was wrong about that, but again, he was wrong in the exact same way so many others are about the color chartreuse represents. Why do so many remember chartreuse as not being just a different color, but the same wrong color? A memory of another timeline that's been altered, or of a parallel world, perhaps? It certainly makes one wonder!

To make a mistake on a color is one thing. People do this. Again, for so many to make the same mistake regarding the same color is an oddity in itself. Furthermore, having them all thinking the same and wrong alternate color was the correct one is just downright weird. Coincidences happen, but these are more synchronicities than coincidences. (We will discuss "synchronicities" a bit later on).

There are more such instances, quite a few, but the point here is these serve to illustrate the Mandela Effect. Tens of thousands, even hundreds of thousands of people remember things as being different in some way than they actually are. Moreover, these differences are often about the same things and they are in error about them in the same exact way.

To add to the enigma, often, such people will have two simultaneous sets of memories concerning the event or instance, as with Mandela dying in the 1980s. However, they also know he died much more recently. How does one account for this peculiarity, as well, this strange duality of memories residing in someone's mind at the same time?

Yes, as I've said, it is possible different people remember different things erroneously and they often do, but for so many to remember things differently, yet in the same alternate way, is just downright bizarre. There is no other way to put it. Could they all then be mistaken and in exactly the same way, making the same error by sheer chance? What would the probability of such a thing be, other than a very low one?

Again, many are so emphatic in the validity of their alternate memories that they seriously believe this to the point they feel there is some sort of, an overt attempt by "someone" or "something" to wipe out and make illegitimate what were once valid memories, at least about some particular point in the past. Many post their views on this in various forums all over the Internet, or even create their own websites on the subject for the same purpose.

Real or not, the so-called Mandela Effect is a force we must reckon with, because it is a real manifestation, whatever the cause. This means there have to be some sort of social implications involved, at the very least. If this many people focus on certain things, and are convinced they remember them differently than others, something appears to be going on that needs investigation, regardless of the cause, because it is a real phenomenon, if only a social one. The interesting part is the fact of why it only concerns certain things and isn't far more general in nature and scope. Why just these things in particular? If faulty memories, they certainly are faulty in a very selective way and with many people being involved in having this same specific fault.

**An Alternate Solution.** There is another interpretation as to the cause of these things, these examples of the Mandela Effect, and it isn't just poor educations and/or poorer memories of thousands of people who all get it wrong in the same way. There is also the idea of parallel universes. As mentioned earlier, there is much scientific evidence and theory to back this idea as being a real one, as we will see in the next chapter. In addition, perhaps, the Mandela Effect is a result of there being such parallel universes, otherwise known as alternate timelines.

If this is so, then the Mandela Effect has a real explanation. People just might be switching back and forth between timelines, ones that are very close in many respects, but not all. Some researchers are convinced this may happen all the time and not just in rare instances that we move back and forth between alternate realities. These "other" realities may be so close to our own, only the random splitting of a single atom versus one not splitting might be the only difference between them.

In short, they say we don't just live in one timeline, but in multiple ones. They simply aren't aware of this fact because they are alike to the point of being virtually identical. That is, most of the time, it seems...sometimes, not.

How then could one know if this was happening? How could you tell if your wife, sister, father, mother, brother, friend or coworkers were mirror images of ones, or the "real" ones you always knew and were born with? Another interesting consequence is that maybe, again according to some proponents of the theory, we really are switching all the time, perhaps sometimes even from second to second. In this case, we have no one "real" version of all these people in our lives at all, but perhaps countless versions of them, instead. Rather a chilling thought, isn't it?

These same proponents argue that timelines as if like strands of spaghetti, not only intertwine, but also may even diverge and then rejoin! In the example given, if one parallel universe is different in just one tiny regard, e.g., an atom that split versus one in ours that did not, and then that atom in ours did subsequently split, then the two universes might be identical again and so merge as one. Again, a strange concept, but one some physicists actually believe might be possible, and in some cases, even probable.

**Conclusion:** What would all this this mean for time travel? What would be the consequences for the concept of what we consider reality? They would not be good ones, I'm afraid. The results of such a thing being true would be virtually incomprehensible for us, for reality and time, as we know it.

Think of the universe that we know as not being static or rigid at all, as we perceive it. Rather, it might be constantly shifting sort of in and out of phase, from one close reality to another close one. Yet, these realities are so much the same, we aren't even aware we are shifting most of the time, except for those few times when the shift is greater and/or we "remember" something as being different than it is, as with the Mandela Effect.

This would mean the person you think of as your father, for example, might instead be an infinite series of such "fathers," all so alike in looks, behavior, history, etc., that you can't usually tell the difference. You would be the same way to him. As his son or daughter, and without him knowing it, you would really be just one of an infinity, or near infinity of "you" that shift back and forth through varying realities, all of which your father erroneously assumes is just the one and the real "you."

As for time travel, it would certainly mean that time travel, at least "sideways" to other timelines would certainly be possible. Furthermore, if someone "slips" into a parallel timeline, not only might people be different, as well as things and places, such as cities and countries that exist and suddenly then don't seem to exist, but such shifts might go farther. What if one entered a timeline that was ahead of our own? What if we entered one that was well behind ours in history? Then we would be experiencing, *de facto*, time travel into the future and the past, if not precisely our own past or future.

This Many Worlds Theory does have a basis in fact. The Inflation Theory of the Universe, the current and most agreed upon theory of how it formed, supports the Many Worlds Theory.

This is because it requires that more than just our universe popped into existence at the instant of the Big Bang. Moreover, a physicist, Hugh Everett III, came up with the theory. He felt it might explain the strange behavior of particles in Quantum Physics. Since then, there have been other physicists, and the number keeps growing, who feel the Many Worlds Theory must be true.

In addition, there are no less than five major theories concerning our type of universe. All say more than one universe or timeline might be possible. In fact, they say this would often be probable, or even as some put it, "necessary." All these theories have real credence, not only in the ideas themselves, the evidence such theories are based on, but also in mathematical support, as well.

What does this mean? Well, it might mean that we may not live in one timeline, but many, many versions of it, and so there are many versions of "us" doing this, as well. We all slip back and forth all the time amongst ourselves, but sometimes, if rarely, going too far, and so experiencing such major changes that we do notice them.

Some versions of us would come to our universe and some go to others. Additionally, in both cases, it might just be that some never return to their timelines, but simply utterly vanish. This is an incredible and again, a frightening concept. Nevertheless, the idea does have its supporters and these aren't "fringe element" supporters either, but again, some mainstream physicists and cosmologists. They might not like this idea, but it could well be a ramification and consequence if their theories concerning the Big Bang of our universe, or even reality itself, as being correct.

One last point and this is on a definitely lighter note. This one is a bit tongue-in-cheek, as well; people often complain about putting two socks into the wash.

However, they only find one when they empty the dryer. Yes, this is funny, but it is so common, many put forth joking explanations about the idea that the pair to a sock may be falling into a parallel universe through the dryer. Authors even write short stories on this subject, it is so common a complaint.

Others claim the same thing when it comes to spotting shoes on the highways. Always, there only seems to be the one shoe! Yes, this is a matter for humor, as well, but the truth is, nobody has ever really explained it. Many of us notice this, to the point it is the subject of jokes by various comedians. Others write about this topic, if often wryly, in various books. We accept these peculiarities, although many have tried to explain, again if humorously, why only the one shoe, and never a pair of them, and the same for those socks.

I have to admit, personally, I can't imagine how people can lose only one shoe on the highway, not notice the fact, and so then go back for it. Furthermore, as most of us have, I've seen many shoes on the highways, but only one at a time.

What if the answer to that riddle isn't quite the joke we think it is... By the way, if you think people don't really wonder about these things, then check out the following webpage. You will find links to multiple discussions and mentions of these odd phenomena, so it is a topic of discussion and sometimes, serious consideration by many:

https://www.google.com/search?q=who+came+up+with+the+Many+Worlds+Theory%3F&ie=utf-8&oe=utf-8#q=only+one+shoe+on+the+highway

Moreover, even Wikipedia has an article on this subject. It says, in part:

*"Abandoned footwear, such as a lone boot or shoe, has often been noted in out-of-the-way places like ponds or by the side of roads.... Sometimes the shoes may even be new and fashionable... The lost slipper in the Cinderella folktale is a classic example of the literary device of the "lost object."*

And the article later goes on to say:

*"The theme of abandoned footwear and their untold story is explored in detail in Julie Ann Shapiro's novel, Jen-Zen and the One Shoe Diaries.... The titular character describes the phenomenon, "The forgotten shoes are everywhere: littering the side of the highway, floating in the tide, going upstream with the salmon, or occupying a field like a dead body, discarded and left to rot."*

So perhaps the subject, although a funny one, has its thoughtful side, as well. In any case, it is just another strange fact of our reality, it seems, and one of the more amusing ones at that. Or is it? The answer to that last question is still unknown, and so just might have to involve parallel realities. Yes, I'm mostly joking here, but not quite completely...

# CHAPTER 12
## Evidence For Time Travel

*"The limitless content of our universe might be only one instance of a large (and possibly infinite) number of other universes."*

— Seth Shostak

As promised, we will now consider yet another type of evidence for time travel, one that requires harder evidence. Again, one may well be surprised at just how much of this sort of evidence there is available, as well. Let's start with a more recent discovery:

**Watch Out Of Time?** This is truly a bizarre thing, and rather inexplicable in some respects, just so strange is this account. In 2008, so quite recently in fact, archaeologists opened a long-buried tomb. This was in the province of Si Quing in China. Inside was a casket. Archaeologists later dated this coffin to being around 400 years old, although some think it is possibly even older than that. Because of the antiquity of the casket, this acted as a verifiable way to determine the date of the tomb itself. After all, the tomb had to have been at least as old as the casket placed within it, if not older.

However, for our purposes here, it isn't the coffin or its contents that are of interest to us. Rather, while excavating in the earth around the coffin, the scientists discovered something that is perhaps unparalleled; they found what looked to be a tiny watch "ring," made of gold. The hands showed the time to be six minutes after ten. Whether this was for the morning or evening is unknown. Etched into the watch was even the make of it, as being of "Swiss" origin.

This watch, or a facsimile of one (without taking apart the watch, one can't be certain), is quite tiny. That the watch was undoubtedly there in the tomb, and at the time, someone sealed the tomb, seems in little doubt. The watch lay buried. It showed signs of interment in this way for a long time, and again, was inside of a sealed and undiscovered tomb. Moreover, the watch could not have been made more than a hundred years ago, and yet the tomb was 400 years old! Somebody had a Swiss watch ring and buried it in a Ming Dynasty tomb? How could this be possible? The idea defies all normal logic.

There is one other thing here; again, nobody has attempted to open the "watch." Therefore, nobody is sure if it actually might turn out to be a real watch, rather than a copy of one without examining the insides, but it does appear to be real. Still, whether or not it truly is, is a question whose answer is yet to be determined.

In either case, it doesn't change things, because how did a much more recent watch or facsimile of a more recent one end up where and "when" it did? In other words, what was it doing in a place and time where it simply shouldn't have been, never have been?

Of course, there are the inevitable claims that the picture is a photo "shopped" hoax. However, since that claim, more pictures of the ring/watch show the watch from different angles. The watch is soiled and encrusted with age, but still certainly visible enough to see that it clearly does look like a watch. Two of the images of the watch are included below.

Furthermore, the person who claimed it was a faked picture offers no proof at all of this claim, but merely states it as if it were a fact, but without any supportive evidence whatsoever. Additionally, the archaeologists involved insist they did find the watch, but cannot account for:

1. How it got there, and,

2. How it can look so old without actually being old. So the questions arise, did someone travel back in time? Did they accidentally drop the watch there? Otherwise, again, how could it have gotten there?

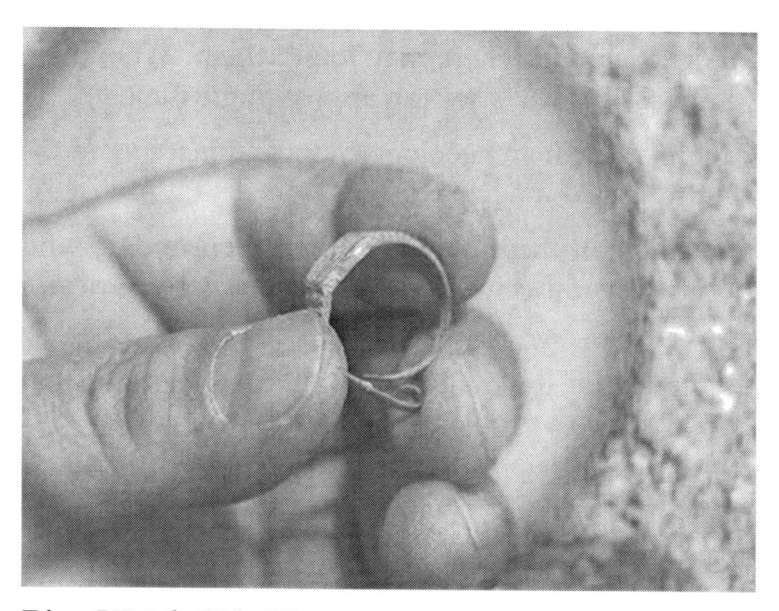

**Ring Watch Side View**

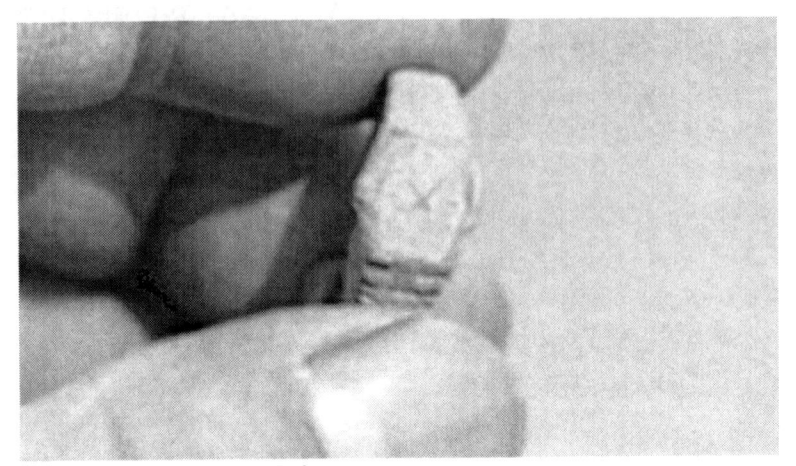

**Ring Watch Front View**

**Conclusion:** When we combine the find of this watch with the other countless objects discovered over the last centuries in their thousands, we face a real conundrum. That is, what do we make of all these objects? How do we account for when and where they found them? Well, there are several possible ways we can approach the issue:

1. We can do as most archaeologists do, and just ignore the matter entirely, as if it never existed.

2. We can claim all these objects in their thousands, found over the last several centuries are just one long series of incredible hoaxes.

3. We can accept the reality that it may just be that "Houston, we have a problem," and try to deal with it.

Let's deal first with the idea of ignoring the objects. This is simply getting harder and harder to do, as more of them appear. Yes, archaeologists have been very good at this ignoring thing for a long time now, but again, as more of these are found, investigated further, and discovered to be real, it becomes harder for archaeology to pretend they just don't exist.

The second point is just absurd in my opinion. Yes, certainly, some oopart finds might be hoaxes, but others being so just makes no rational sense whatsoever. How does one account for thousands of Nano screws, for instance? These were dug up along an entire river and one of its tributary lengths, screws that have been determined to have been buried for thousands of years, at least, and ones humans simply could not have been capable of making in such primitive times?

The metal, titanium, is in some of the screws. The ability to refine this metal is a much more recent and modern accomplishment, since extraordinarily high temperatures are required in the process. Furthermore, to make something so small is also a recent accomplishment. Prior to the 1980's even our civilization's abilities to create nano objects was almost nonexistent!

Besides this, there is the matter of finding real objects embedded in coal, stone, dug up at deep levels, sometimes in actual archaeological-administered digs, etc. How does one account for these via a normal explanation?

The third point, of dealing with these objects is the most pragmatic and so practical approach. This does mean we might have to reorganize and so change our viewpoint of historical events on this planet and sometimes in truly major ways. Still, we must do this if we truly want to further science, discover what has really been going on in our past. "Somebody" has left a large number of objects in times where they shouldn't have.

Our civilization couldn't have made them at such distant times in the past, and in some cases, would have trouble making them even now. So just who did? We should be trying to find the answers to these mysterious oopart objects so we can find out just who left them behind.

In other words, again to paraphrase the astronauts with regard to Houston, "we should try to find a solution." We might not like what we find, but at least, we will be closer to the truth and isn't that what science is supposed to be all about in the final analysis? We shouldn't try to be making our history conform to preset notions of archaeologists. Rather, they should be trying to find out what our real history was all about.

# CHAPTER 13
# "Chrononauts and Time Slips

*"The time-space age has begun."*

— Andrew D. Basiago

This quotation of Andrew Basiago is here for a reason. The man, a lawyer by initial trade, made some startling claims and ones he still insists are true. For one thing, Mr. Basiago claims to be a chrononaut (a sort of time traveler, but one that travels through space, as well as through time, apparently). He makes the statement that time travel is real, and was originally a part of the expanded "Philadelphia Experiment" of legendary and movie fame, as well.

The chrononauts' abilities, according to him, included the technique instantaneously to transport themselves and things to such distant locations as Mars via teleportation. He also insists that "remote sensing," the ability to see things at a far distance with only one's mind is real, as well. He states the military has been involved in such experiments for some time now, decades, it seems.

Mr. Basiago is certainly right about one thing; the idea of remote sensing is not new. Even movies have mentioned it, such as George Clooney in *The Men Who Stare at Goats*, a 2009 comedy/drama, is just one example. This was a fanciful film, but based on a nonfiction book by Author Jon Ronson and his investigation of such activities by the American military. He explored their sojourn into the idea of developing soldiers to have psychic abilities. Their purpose was to develop these soldiers as tools for spying and as weapons, also. Even the movie, at the very end, states there is more truth to the events depicted within the film than one might suppose, but does not then elaborate on this. There are other movies on this subject, as well as books.

Mr. Basiago further states that in the decades of the 1960s and 1970s, a number of children, 140 in all, were in a special project by the government organization, DARPA. Mr. Basiago was one of these children, according to him. The name of the endeavor was supposedly the Project Pegasus. Additionally, Andrew Basiago insists the project utilized documents by Nikola Tesla, secret ones, and with regard specifically to "radiant energy." This, according again to Mr. Basiago, was capable of creating a method of teleportation. He explained the process allowed for the bending of spacetime, and so could work for such purposes as teleportation.

He went on to say this wasn't just for short hops, either. People could go much farther. They could even go to other planets, including Mars, as well, as mentioned above.

What is the upshot of all this? Well, the kid chrononauts were instrumental through this means in helping to establish human bases on Mars and perhaps elsewhere, according to Mr. Basiago. Children, it seems, were ideal for teleporting purposes as opposed to adults, because being younger, they could better handle the rigors of the teleportation process, being more mentally flexible.

Mr. Basiago also stated they were capable of using tunnels (reminiscent of the television series, *The Time Tunnel?*) and in combination with a type of holographic technology, the children could travel to parallel realities. In some instances, these realities were behind ours in their timelines, so were effectively in the past. This, again according to Mr. Basiago, made sure that no terrible time paradoxes could occur, as in someone killing their own grandfather (Grandfather Paradox), for instance and thus never having been born, since they traveled back in time to other timelines, but not our own.

Mr. Basiago goes further. He insists there is photographic evidence of all this being true. For example, he says there is a photograph of Abraham Lincoln, one taken just days before his assassination. The photo includes a picture of Mr. Basiago as a child. This was when he was still a member of the project.

Now, whether all this is true is a matter of whether one believes Mr. Basiago, or not, except of course, for the photograph, which would seem to lend some credence to the man's claims. However, the child in the photograph, although looking somewhat modern in appearance, also fits the times, as well.

The haircuts are the same as the other children in the photograph. The clothing, although appearing somewhat different, is not so different as to really stand out. Furthermore, the shoes seem in keeping with the period. Was he then dressed to fit the period to which he traveled? He could well have been, one supposes.

There is another interesting aspect to all this. As with the caller on George Noory's Coast-To-Coast Radio who said, "black-eyed" children who forced him to travel backward and forward through time in a sort of seesaw motion. Could these black-eyed children be the ones of Project Pegasus? If so, then they may have learned to time travel without the help of the government...

Image of Basiago as a child in the past?

**Photograph of Basiago In Civil War Times.**

All this may sound rather unbelievable, but there is some more evidence to support the idea that time travel might well be happening. This comes from a scientist who makes that exact claim. Masao Ninomiya has publicly announced that he thinks there is outside interference with the Large Hadron Collider at CERN. He bases this belief on the fact that M-Theory, often described as "the theory of everything" in physics, does allow for time travel. Moreover, indeed, the theory in actuality does allow for this. Therefore, this much is true, at least with regard to his idea.

He also believes a particle capable of traveling in time, the Higgs "singlet," does exist (Please see chapter on quantum physics for more information on this particle.) However, he believes "someone" is deliberately thwarting our attempts to find this particle and/or use it for time travel purposes. Mr. Ninomiya points to the constant problems and delays in the use of the Large Hadron Collider as possible proof of this happening, or at least it being delayed until a time when it is "okay' for the collider to be allowed to work and so then discover the Higgs singlet.

*"It is as if something is going back in time to keep the universe from being hit by a bus."*

This is the way the physicist, himself, puts it, with regard to the blocking of our attempts in getting a handle on the existence and/or use of the Higgs singlet. He thinks someone or something is denying us the right to explore this field. This "someone" is in the future.

As bizarre as this might first seem to sound, remember, this is a physicist saying this. Furthermore, there is another and very strange correlation to this whole idea. A man by the name of Eloi Cole was in the CERN facilities illegally and so promptly arrested. This took place in 2010.

He claims he was sent back from the future to that time in Switzerland and his purpose there was to sabotage the Large Hadron Collider to keep it from functioning at that point in time. He made other claims, as well, as in for example that in his time; the concept of countries was no more.

What makes this story especially curious is something that happened a short time later. Eloi Cole subsequently vanished from a mental facility where they had incarcerated him for his trespass and bizarre claims as to why he had done this. This was in Geneva, Switzerland, and his disappearance was without a trace.

Where he went, or how he might have escaped is unknown, but one thing is certain, and that is no one has seen him since. This does make one wonder if he might have disappeared to an "any when" rather than an "anywhere," as a result. Again, this is a truly odd tale with a weird ending.

Yet, it does seem to lend some credence to the idea that perhaps the LHC suffers interference from the future, and this interference is in order to stop the Higgs singlet discovery, at least, for now. To this day, we have yet to discover that particle.

Large Hadron Collider

**Conclusion:** A scientist who has a real fear people from the future might be interfering with the LHC. A lawyer who claims to be part of a former group of time traveling children? This seems like the stuff of pure science fiction, but apparently, it is not.

To top all this off, we even have one who claims he was a time traveler and then subsequently vanished without a trace, but only after trying actively to interfere with the functioning of the Large Hadron Collider at CERN.

What then are we to make of all of this? Are these people just insane, misguided, or hoax perpetrators, or are they telling the truth? Just how did the one man disappear from a mental facility and nobody ever saw him again? Why would another man, an intelligent one who was capable of passing his bar exams to become an attorney, make such wild claims?

Why would a physicist go out on such a far limb to claim our present could be the subject of interference by someone or something from the future, risking real damage to his professional reputation to do so? Moreover, other physicists at the Large Hadron Collider, as well, also hold out hopes for the Higgs singlet, a particle that might just be a time traveler in its own right, as actually existing.

One conclusion we can draw from all of this. Time is certainly not the hard and fixed "thing" we once thought it was, nor are attitudes about whether one can travel through it, either. On the contrary, time seems to be a fluid thing, even as viewpoints on traveling through it are. Time is not some static, an unchangeable thing as we once thought, but rather seems capable of much we hadn't even once contemplated as possible.

If that's the case and it certainly seems to be, then all bets on whether not only if time travel is possible, but also if it is already happening are off. It may very well be happening and someone is interfering with our timeline right now, and in perhaps more than one way! Based on the evidence, I think this might be likely.

# CHAPTER 14

# Rendelsham Incident--Time Travelers From The Future?

*"As scientists, we track down all promising leads, and there's reason to suspect that our universe may be one of many - a single bubble in a huge bubble bath of other universes."*

— Brian Greene,

**Theoretical and String Theory Physicist**

Now we come to a topic one might think has no place here in such a book as this, given the fact the subject matter is time travel. Still, this topic does pertain to time travel in many ways. In addition, this is in more ways than many might think and perhaps profoundly so.

Just what am I talking about here? Well, nothing less than binary code, the basic code of all computer languages, and a special message received in such a code. Furthermore, the main participant in this event feels certain this isn't an alien visitation, but rather one from the future.

The idea binary code somehow ties into time travel is a recent one. Furthermore, this came about for a number of reasons, but there were two main ones. The first one is, oddly, a rather famous UFO incident. This took place in the Rendlesham Forest encounter in England.

We won't go into detail about this here, as many have seen or read about this particular incident many times. In fact, Rendlesham is one of the more famous UFO encounters. However, for those not familiar with it, here are the basic facts of the event:

In 1980, in December of that year, Jim Penniston, an American sergeant, along with other military members, had to check out an unidentified flying object that had appeared late one night near the Air Force Base. This, they promptly did.

Making their way through the woods, they saw a hazy sort of light in the distance, off amongst the trees. As they approached the source, Sergeant Penniston thought they might be dealing with some sort of crashed small aircraft. At that point, he assumed this would just be a plane of the more mundane variety. This idea of his, was soon to change and dramatically so.

Upon arrival upon the scene, Penniston quickly realized what he was seeing was no downed Cessna, but a flying vehicle, one of a type he had never seen before. In addition, remember, his knowledge of aircraft was extensive, being a long-time member of the U.S. Air Force. He had intimate knowledge of all the different types of aircraft they had.

The craft in this case was not large. The shape was triangular and the thing had a dark, shiny, outer hull, made of what seemed a glass-like material, or perhaps a highly polished metal of some sort. There were lights arranged around the object at regular intervals and these flashed red and blue.

Other than this, the craft was rather featureless, for it had no windows, landing real gear apparatus, or anything else of this nature. There was what appeared to be some sort of arcane writing across the surface in one area, which Penniston would later describe as being of a "hieroglyphic" nature.

Assuming he must be seeing some sort of classified, government-sponsored, black-project aircraft, Penniston approached the vehicle, if very slowly and carefully. Upon closer inspection, the sergeant realized his notion of this being a secret prototype vehicle of his government's devising was highly unlikely. Besides the bizarre shape and nature of the craft, which he had never seen before, there was also the weird effect of its presence on the immediate local environment.

All natural sounds he'd been hearing while he and his team had been making their way through the woods were now gone. They not only stopped, but it was as if his team being this close to the aircraft somehow suppressed them. There was also a feeling of electrical charge in the air near the thing, as if some sort of static electric field was in play.

Here is where an even weirder statement of Penniston's comes into the story; he would later describe the sensation of being close to the alien vehicle (for that's how he then thought of it), as causing a "dragging of time." This sensation later found support by the fact that after having left the area, he and his crew realized their watches were all off. Although only a few minutes seemed to have passed for them subjectively at the site, in fact, the duration had been more like several hours!

The tale of these men does not end with this astounding discovery. The sergeant had gone up to the craft and even touched its hull at one point, the better to determine the material making up the surface of the flying vehicle. He reported a peculiar feeling of something invading and flooding his thoughts when he did this. Later that night, after returning to base (the vehicle having since taken off), and completing his report for his superiors, Sergeant Penniston, exhausted, finally retired for the night.

While he slept, he dreamed of "ones and zeros" streaming through his mind. He would wake up, go to sleep, and the zeros and ones would continue to flow. He couldn't shake this recurring dream of them, no matter how he tried.

The ones and zeroes were binary code, as it turned out (according to Sergeant Penniston), because he ended up by writing a notebook, filling the pages with the numbers he couldn't get out of his head, and in the sequence he kept mentally visualizing them.

Later, when planning to appear on *Ancient Aliens*, a popular television series, he, along with help from the appropriate experts, had the binary code translated. As it turned out, it wasn't just mental "gibberish," as Penniston had once thought, but rather translated into what appeared to be a short statement about the "exploration of Humanity," followed by some numbers and what seemed to be planetary coordinates here on Earth, a series of them.

Besides the list of coordinates, there was the following:

"Origin 52.0942532N 13.131269W

*Origin Year 8100."*

Please take special notice of the phrase, "Origin Year." It says, "8100." This puts the date of origin of the ship, presumably, over *six thousand years* into the future! That is if, of course, those controlling the ship were using our dating system, which according to the translators, seemed likely, given the context of the other coordinates being real places on Earth, etc., and utilizing the same basis for interpretation of the code. If the coordinates were the same as ours, why wouldn't the dating system be, as well, was their feeling.

Since the other coordinates identified real places, such as Belize, Caracol, the area of the Great Pyramids in Egypt, a temple site in Greece, etc., as well as the location of a supposedly mythical island, Hy-Brazil, there was, needless to say, consternation at the results of this translation effort. However, this consternation was even more so with regard to the date.

This one thing caused Sergeant Penniston and the experts to rethink the idea the "UFO" was from an alien race from outer space. There was now a good chance the craft was from Earth, but an Earth thousands of years into the future!

Was it a craft from a future time? The date mentioned in the translation of the binary code would seem to indicate this. Did someone reach back through time to deliver some sort of information to us of the present? Were the future beings who controlled the ship our human descendants or "something" else?

Some of these questions are not possible to answer at present, but if UFOs (all or some) are from the future, it would explain much about worldwide sightings of them if they, indeed, were exploring today's humanity and current events. For instance, it would account for:

**1.** Why people are being abducted, not so much to be experimented on and changed, but simply to gather information through physical examinations of our current physiognomy.

**2.** Why so often UFOs appear near military/nuclear bases, not to mention ships carrying nuclear armaments at sea, including many of America's aircraft carriers. They could have a strong interest in our current military level of technology, deployments, etc. It is quite conceivable that over the intervening thousands of years, many such details could have been lost to them, our possible descendants.

**3.** Why the interest UFOs seem to have in our space program, such as following the original moon landing trip, the Apollo 11 mission and so many other of our space explorations. Here they would have the same motivations, to learn more about the details of our accomplishments of this time.

In other words, it would all be about gathering data of our time and all the different aspects of our present-day world. Again, this would give an excellent reason for the appearance of UFOs in our skies. Instead of aliens, it could well be our future "us," our own descendants doing this, trying to learn more about their own past.

Alternatively, it might be something else from the future. Many experts predict humanity, as we know it, is on the verge of becoming extinct in just a matter of decades or even less. Even the famous scientist, Stephen Hawking, recently issued a bleak warning about the danger of artificial intelligences of our own creation taking over the world, and of us then becoming extinct as a species.

Other scientists go so far as to say we are on the brink of new types of humans entirely, superior ones that are super-enhanced through genetic engineering, and/or incorporating cybernetic technology into them as a physical and integral part of their makeup. So although perhaps "they" are from the future, sadly, we have no guarantee UFOs are from "our" future, or at least, not the one we envision for ourselves now...

There is one alternative to this here and it is a truly dark one. Perhaps some great catastrophe or cataclysm is in the offing, our near future. If so, much information about our existence and time here on Earth would inevitably be lost. Future survivors with time-travel capabilities would then have to come back in time. That is, they would if they wanted to learn more about us and maybe the events leading up to the holocaust, if for instance, it turns out to be a coming nuclear war. Again, a very dark but still very possible idea, even so.

The reason I mention this is the phrase the UFO used when "speaking" to the sergeant. The phrase "exploration of Humanity," is a rather chilling one. Human descendants wouldn't likely refer to us in this time in that way. Being human themselves, they wouldn't need to state such a thing about us. It's almost as if whoever is saying this isn't human, themselves, and that perhaps we are one of many "other" species they are exploring, and so the term.

With regard to the Rendlesham incident, one must also ask why certain places were marked as coordinates. Moreover, why was this information then passed on to Sergeant Penniston by mental means? Was this just an error, a mistake that he had tapped into something he wasn't supposed to have by accident, or was it a deliberate message to us humans? Nevertheless, why this information? In particular, for example, is the fact of the coordinates for the mysterious island of Hy-Brazil.

This is supposedly a mythical island to the west of Ireland. Nevertheless, for a fantasy island, it had a long life on various maps as an actual and real place. Depictions of the island stayed on maps well into the late 1800s and had appeared so on maps for centuries!

The first mention of the island seems to have been as a place called "Bracile" on a map made in 1325 CE. Angelino Dulcert created the chart and it showed the island in the North Atlantic, west of Ireland.

In 1436 CE, Hy-Brasil appeared on yet another chart, this time one created by the Venetian cartographer, Andrea Bianco. Now the island had the name "Insula de Brasil. The mysterious island's debut on maps didn't stop here. The place showed up yet once more, this time on a Catalan navigational map. This was in 1480 CE. The name had changed only slightly this time to calling the island, "Illa de Brasil." In addition, the location altered marginally, moving a little further to the south and west of the western Irish coast.

Some maps even depicted not only the shape of the island (roughly circular), but also showed a river, or perhaps a strait horizontally bisecting the island on an east-west basis. Depictions of the island on maps continued. Yet once more, the island appeared on another map, this time in 1865, at the end of the American Civil War. Moreover, the position was still to the south and west of Ireland on this chart.

There were numerous reports of sightings of this "Hy-Brazil," as well, by various ships, or so the ships' captains and crews claimed. Therefore, not only was the island on numerous maps for centuries, but apparently numerous ships' crews, as well, sighted the place over those same centuries.

Yet now, we have no such island on our maps, both manmade and/or satellite in origin. It seems Hy-Brazil has vanished, even as others have. Nobody now sees the island, either. So what happened to Hy-Brazil? Was it ever there, and if so, did it just vanish? That last would seem highly unlikely, and yet, we have a very current case of just this sort of thing happening!

An island has disappeared very recently, it seems, if one goes by the maps of the western Pacific Ocean. This mysterious disappearance of an isle is all too reminiscent of Hy-Brasil. Maps repeatedly showed Sandy Island as being there, and for a couple of centuries, at least. Various ships and their crews sighted the island and/or "rediscovered it" over this long interval of time.

Yet, now the island appears to have vanished. Yes, various explanations abound for the disappearance of Sandy Island and they are identical to the ones given for the disappearance of Hy-Brazil, such as an older map had been wrong and the newer ones made from it had repeatedly incorporated the mistake.

As for people seeing the island, the explanation is that ships' crews mistook a floating patch of pumice stones for a land mass. That floating patch of pumice stones seems to have hung around in one area for a very long time if this is so. One would have thought random ocean currents would have moved or dispersed it over two full centuries! Moreover, it is not there now, and nobody has ever claimed to see such a thing.

Regardless of its current disappearance, passing ships spotted Sandy Island multiple times through the last couple of centuries. Furthermore, these were ships flying the flags of various countries.

Again, some argue the island never existed. However and strangely, even a Google Earth Map shows a satellite image of Sandy Island being there. Nonetheless, the map shows the island as redacted by being "blacked out with pixilation," but even the shape of the island is still obvious from the image. The pixilation conforms to what appears to be the natural outline of an island.

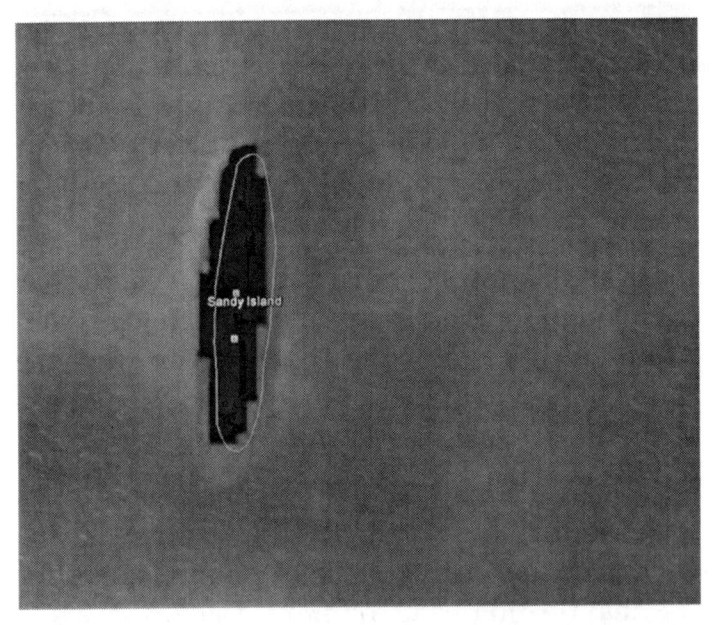

**Pixelated Image of Sandy Island On Google Earth Map. Notice odd shape of pixilation? It's not just rectangular.**

What was the satellite photo showing if there was no island there? Moreover, why was it not only redacted, but also the redaction/pixilation was in the shape of a narrow, north-south island, even as other charts had shown the shape of the island to be?

Normally, Google only redacts photo images of military and high-security institutions at governments' requests, yet they redacted Sandy Island, as well. Why? If there was no island there to begin with, what was there to hide in the satellite photo of the Google Earth Map, but ocean? A strange situation at best and one that rightly gives rise to a number of questions and even some conspiracy theories, as a result.

Accordingly, the UFO's coordinates that seem to indicate the position of a now vanished Hy-Brasil are not as bizarre as some might think, because even though we cannot "see" the island now, it doesn't mean that it wasn't there at some time in the past. For a time-traveling UFO, a visit to the place would have been no problem, apparently.

The question is, if the island did once exist, and it isn't now "cloaked" in invisibility as some legends and conspiracy theorists think, then just what happened to Hy-Brasil? Well, one answer is a possible cataclysmic geological event. The area of the Atlantic where Hy-Brasil is supposed to be, or have been, is close to the Mid-Atlantic Ridge, a highly geologically active area, one known for frequent earthquakes and volcanos, both on land and on the sea floor. One only has to look at the constant and violent eruptions of volcanoes in Iceland, also on the Mid-Atlantic Ridge, to see the effects of this geological instability.

Did Hy-Brazil vanish as the result of an explosive volcano of the caldera type, as have other islands in the past? Did Hy-Brazil share the fate of Krakatoa and/or Thera, the last also referred to in current times as Santorini? Was the UFO referring to a place that was once real, but is no more? Alternatively, is it there but just now somehow cloaked in invisibility?

Again, we can only conjecture as to why certain location coordinates in the binary code translation of the Rendlesham UFO were there. As to their real purpose, why the thing was mentally reciting them, is a question. At this time, nobody knows the answer, just as nobody knows why the sergeant was the one to receive this binary code. Why choose him? Alternatively, did they choose him? Did he just stumble, perhaps, upon the information, just being the one to first approach the craft?

Nobody seems to be able to answer these questions, other than to supply additional suppositions. For example, one can suppose it wouldn't have had necessarily to be the sergeant, but rather anyone who might have chosen to touch the hull of the Rendlesham UFO on that night. Possibly, the UFO was ready and willing to transmit the message to anyone who approached it.

Instead, perhaps nobody was supposed to know the code. Perhaps the UFO had a mechanical failure and this failure forced it to land? Maybe, it wasn't meant to be in the forest at all that night. Was it being there a mistake? If so, did Sergeant Penniston accidentally eavesdrop on a mental transmission not meant for him to hear at all? That, too, is possible.

Nevertheless, we must remember it is Professor Ron Mallet's belief that if there is one thing that might be possible to send back through time, if nothing else, that something might be information. This is what Sergeant Penniston received, information. Of course, there is the matter of the UFO being a time ship, as well, which could well mean more than just information is capable of traveling through time.

Another theory is the UFO might have come from an alternate timeline, which is ahead of our own, and so "crossed over" from a parallel universe. In the process, the craft also transferred itself back in time, since our timeline was thousands of years behind its own. Again, nobody can know this for sure, at least, not yet. Still some researchers do think this would be a more likely scenario. They feel that if one could travel back in time and make any alterations that again, this would "instantly" create a new parallel universe where things then progressed differently from that point forward. We could be that new timeline as a result. Our future could now be different from what it once might have been before the arrival of the Rendlesham UFO.

**Conclusion:** All such suppositions aside, what is important here is that a famous tale, one well documented, witnessed by a number of members of the military as a group, one with even a recording to corroborate part of the event, did actually take place. The interpretation of the binary code Sergeant Penniston claims to have received also seems to have some evidence to support it. This is because the translations of the code made actual sense and were not just garbage, or something unrecognizable and having no syntax to it at all.

Therefore, that the Rendlesham incident was a real event is pretty much a given at this point. The recording is also verifiable. As for the sergeant receiving binary code, that is less verifiable, but it ties in very neatly with something recently discovered by a mainstream scientist and easily confirmed by other such scientists.

Additionally, this scientist's weird discovery does seem to lend some credence to the idea of binary code being something "everyone" would use and for a very simple reason. The thing is, you see, binary code might just be an innate part of everything, even the very basis for the existence of our universe, as we shall see in the next chapter. We will also see how it affects the idea of time travel.

# CHAPTER 15

# Binary Code, The Very Matrix Of Our Universe And Time Travel?

*"This is a war universe. War all the time. That is its nature. There may be other universes based on all sorts of other principles, but ours seems to be based on war and games.*

—**William S. Burroughs**

The above quotation is a rather chilling one, isn't it? Yet, it seems all too true. Life may abound on our world, but it only survives by killing and eating other life, and all the time! This is true from the smallest forms of life, such as viruses and bacteria, clear up to the current top of the food chain, meaning us.

Nothing seems exempt. Even viruses are parasites. They use hosts to survive, often killing those hosts in the process. Bacteria eat each other and us at times, even as insects eat plants, animals eat insects, and we eat those animals. That is, if they aren't already eaten by each other, first.

The next time you look out at your garden, just remember, you aren't seeing a piece of earthly paradise. What you are really looking at, if only you could see it, is a place of constant murder and kill-or-be-killed survival. In others words, that garden really is a "jungle out there" and in every sense of the term, even the darkest one.

Furthermore, our universe is a violent place, as well, so it mirrors life and death on our world in the same way. Death and destruction rules the day with explosive novae incomprehensibly huge supernovas, titanic hypernovas, deadly cosmic ray bursts that span hundreds of light years, planets crashing into each other (even ancient Earth experienced this), colliding black holes, galaxies smashing together, colliding neutron stars…well, the list goes on and on.

Our galaxy is rife with incomprehensibly massive explosions and eruptions occurring all the time. These disruptions repeat throughout all the billions of galaxies in the cosmos, as we know it. Whole solar systems literally are put to the sword every day. Even entire galaxies disintegrate, casting their myriad suns and worlds in every direction, many into the outer darkness of the cold and eternal void of intergalactic space.

Therefore, nobody can rationally argue against Mr. Burroughs quotation, for our world, our very universe is really as a place of "war and games."

This has special significance for us here, because also in our world are the game makers. Whether elaborate or simple, computer-based or board games, these simulations often involve conflict, battles, destruction, and wars. Game makers create all. In other words, when we create simulated worlds to play in, it seems far more often than not, they are violent ones, just as our universe is. Therefore, the question arises, since we do this, might "others" do this, as well. Are there godlike game makers at play here in our universe?

Most of us have seen the movie, *The Matrix*, and its sequels, so the idea of humanity living in a false universe, one created by "others" is hardly a new notion. Yet, there is now real evidence, and from several scientific sources, that this might actually be true in fact, and not just in fiction. For instance:

1. Just as in a computer game, scientists have discovered our universe pixelates on the very small scale, just as computer simulations do. In other words, if we delve down into the smaller and smaller, the universe stops being "solid" and becomes particles, which in turn appear to be manifestations of "strings" vibrating. The way the string vibrates (Superstring Theory), determines the type of particle. In other words, what appears to be real and solid is actually not at all. It only seems to be "real."

2. Additionally, we are like ghosts. That means that we, along with everything else made of matter, are almost entirely made of nothing! In fact, we ourselves, our bodies, are composed of 99.999999999999 percent empty space! That's about as close to 100 percent as anyone can get without actually being precisely there. In addition, remember, the particles that make up that remaining .0000000000001 percent are actually just manifestations of string vibrations, which aren't "solid" either. We are, in short, just a collection of various vibrations, it seems.

The only thing that keeps us from passing through other so-called solid objects as ghosts are supposed to do, is the fact atoms, although almost entirely empty space, have an "electron shell," a cloud of electrons in various states of probability surrounding them. This produces a repulsive force. This repulsion makes a desk feel solid to the touch and keeps one's hand from passing right through it, or vice versa, with the desk going through the hand.

Why is any of this important to our discussion of time travel? Because, as we shall see in a later chapter, time does not seem to exist on the truly microscopic (quantum) level of reality, or if it does, it behaves most strangely, indeed.

We used to think this strangeness of matter and time was limited to that extremely small scale of things, the world of subatomic particles. However, as we shall also see in a later chapter, that doesn't seem to be quite the case. Moreover, if such fluctuations on the quantum level of reality occur on the macroscopic level of reality (our level of reality—the world around us as we see and know it), then those fluctuations very well could include time distortions, time displacements, etc., as well. In other words, time might not really be what we think it is at all, not even on our level of reality.

**3.** Many physicists are also convinced that mathematics don't just describe the universe, but *are* the universe. As one renowned scientist and cosmologist, Max Tegmark, put in 2014, all particles that make up our reality have qualities attached to them. These qualities or properties include such things as "charge and spin."

Yet, these are not real, but rather are just mathematical concepts in their nature. Therefore, it is Max Tegmark's contention that the entire universe and everything in it is just one vast mathematical concept, an elaborate house of cards built out of information and mathematics only.

He partly bases this contention on a fundamental principle of physics. This is no information can be destroyed in the universe, not even the information of an object entering a black hole.

Stephen Hawking stated this with his recent theory of how such information about an object can be, and has to be preserved. After all, if the universe is mathematics or information, one can't go about destroying bits of it here and there without the whole house of cards eventually tumbling down.

There does seem to be scientific evidence to support the idea that the universe is, at its fundamental level, just information. For one thing, we have been able to actually teleport particles. Furthermore, we've done more than teleport those. We've also managed to teleport a simple atom, a whole one!

Now, as incredible as this is, to be able to teleport anything at all, even something more astounding is involved. That is, when we teleport a particle or atom (and soon groups of atoms, as in objects?), it isn't the actual particle or atom itself we are teleporting, but rather just *the information!* The description of the particle travels to the other end, and so the identical particle forms. This is not a different particle, a clone, or twin, but that same particle! Additionally, it is the information, the "quantum state" that is only sent. Physicists refer to this as "quantum teleportation."

There is one proviso to this form of quantum teleportation. Since we are using "classical" methods to send the information, it cannot go faster than the speed of light. Therefore, the teleportation process is not instantaneous, but rather limited by this factor, the speed of light.

The point here isn't to get lost in quantum teleportation and all its subtleties, but rather just to illustrate that the universe may truly be, indeed, just information. What this means is that very much like a computer simulation, which may include buildings, people, plants, cars, dogs, etc., in a game, but aren't really there at all, so too, our universe might be the same.

We very well could just be streams of information that creates the appearance of all this. Doesn't this sound just like the premise for the movies of *The Matrix* series? It would seem to... So are we a computer simulation? The chances, as we shall see below, are good that we are:

**Are We A Simulation?** If our future descendants create simulations, the chances are very great that we are one of them. A good take on this theory is the movie, *The Thirteenth Floor*. In this movie, a group of researchers work to create a great game simulation of 1940's Los Angeles, one people can actually "enter" as if physically, by hooking themselves into the computer and so experiencing the era as if it were real, not only for them, but also for the characters created in the simulation. They, too, would believe they are real. What the researchers don't suspect is that they, themselves, are also a simulation of a future society, so they are creating a simulation within a simulation. It is a very realistic one, but one that is just a computer-generated "game" in reality, and nothing more.

Is this likely to be true for our universe and us? Are we just such a simulation? It might well be, because just as computer games are massive and use elaborate strings of binary computer code, scientists seem to have discovered something recently about our universe in this respect, as well.

**The Universe Seems To Have Actual Binary Code Embedded In The Formulas For It.** The same type of binary code as several major Internet search engines use, including Google's search engine, are "built in" to the formulas for String Theory, which forms the current popular "theory of everything."

A scientist discovered this fact about binary code being in there not long ago and it has caused immense interest and not just a little trepidation and anxiety. Moreover, it isn't just binary code, but the actual finished code for the exact same type of algorithms as used in search engines, such as Yahoo!

What does all this mean for time travel? Well, if our universe is a simulation and perhaps just one of countless other such simulations, then those "others" most likely designed it so that whoever or whatever they might be, they can enjoy the "game" in all its various aspects. In other words, the chances are actually much better than good that we might just be a simulation created by our descendants or whoever. Those who have managed to develop more powerful computers than we have now would be capable of doing this. As Robert Lanza, a noted author on life and consciousness, as well as being a scientist and doctor, said:

*"Sometime in the future, science will be able to create realities that we can't even begin to imagine. As we evolve, we'll be able to construct other information systems that correspond to other realities..."* (Please see *"References"* at end of this book for a link to Robert Lanza's book, *Biocentrism: How Life and Consciousness are the Keys to Understanding the True Nature of the Univere.*)

Moreover, it is highly unlikely such simulation creators would be restricted to just observing the simulations, any more than our game players are restricted to just watching a game unfold without them being an active participant in it. Like most game players here on Earth today, those "other" game players in the future would have the power to observe, but also even to interact with us in multiple ways *and in multiple times!*

Additionally, it is unlikely they would restrict themselves with regard to choosing which time they wished to interact in, meaning they could move forward or backward as they chose in the game, just as we have scenarios set in different "worlds" and times in our games. In short, they would be fully capable of time traveling.

Is this idea of us being a simulation plausible? Yes, I'm afraid so. Nick Bostrom, a resident professor of philosophy at the University of Oxford, no less, came up with a reliable formula for examining the whole question of the possibility of our universe just being a simulation. The formula, after some simple mathematical massaging, shows that, as a PBS article, among others, put it:

$$\text{Probability you are a simulated mind} = \frac{\text{Number of simulations}}{\text{Number of simulations}+1}$$

(See *"References"* at end of book for a link to the PBS website with this article.)

It is not my intention to overwhelm the reader with mathematics, so we won't go into detail on this, because swamping the reader with mathematical formulas is not the premise or reason for this book. However, it should be mentioned, at least in passing, that this formula is based on the idea that the total number of simulations possible or probable is dependent on the number of real minds that exist in the future at the time the simulations are created. Furthermore, the formula also uses how many multiple simulations were made of them.

Remember, all such simulations would be the product of a civilization in the future. It would be a "post-human" one, as the article states, meaning in this case, our descendants or some "others" doing the simulation creating. They would have tremendous computing power and so could do this. Can they achieve such computing power? It seems they can, yes, and given time would do just that.

If one uses Moore's law of how computer power advances, and it has worked for us so far, the day of such computing power is not even far off! Moore's Law states that computing power has doubled approximately every two years. This is incredibly fast and if it continues, we will reach unbelievable levels of computing power in just a decade or two more. We already have reached such comparable levels to computers of just twenty years ago. For example, the Apollo 11 mission's onboard computer was no more powerful than the common pocket calculator of today!

So what would our computers be like in fifty years, a hundred, or even a thousand? It would be unimaginable, one supposes, by today's standards with regard to how far their computer power could go, what their computers would then be capable of doing. Creating simulated universes could well be relatively easy for such potent creatures to accomplish.

Now, how does this affect the probability we are a simulation and nothing more? What does the formula stated above actually show us? Well, that depends on certain factors, and they are:

1. If there are no or at least very few descendant civilizations of species (remember, there may be more than just "us" in this universe, or may not be…),

2. Very few of those civilizations care to run such simulations, or

3. There are such civilizations and they do like to run simulations.

Therefore, if there are no or very few descendants of us, or any "others," or if they have no urge to run such simulations, then we are most likely not a simulation. Nevertheless, if there are any civilizations at all (here or elsewhere), in the future that have any interest in running such simulations, then the probability we are a simulation is quite high, very high.

In fact, it is more likely by far that we are a simulation than not! This is especially so, since simulated civilizations in computers could also become capable of running their own simulations, as well. Again, you could have "nested" simulations within simulations.

How could we know if this is true, if we are such a simulation? Well, just as with the *Matrix* movie series, we might expect small "glitches" in the matrix at times. These would be in the makeup of our universe, and would manifest themselves in ways that would show us the universe has such glitches, as in slight changes in how physics might behave, or for our purposes, how time might behave.

John D. Barrow, a scientist and cosmologist of great repute, came up with this idea. He argued that since our descendants' understanding of the universe might not be total, their programed simulations, meaning our universe for one, would then have some inherent flaws in their makeup. So does our universe have these? Well, we'll explore that in the next chapter.

There is one other thing I should mention more than in just passing here. Earlier, I mentioned that a scientist came up with the fact that binary code exists in the mathematical formulas used for the idea of "super symmetry/string theory."

Again, this is a basic, fundamental theory that attempts to explain the universe mathematically in its totality and is the one most accepted by physicists right now. James Gates, a theoretical physicist, and since then others, as well, have discovered for certain that there is binary code nested in the formulas supporting the idea of super symmetry and string theory. So that such code does exist is a given.

Mind you, they didn't just find binary code of a sort, but again, rather, a very specific and oddly familiar binary code. In short, **they found Block Linear Self Dual Error Correcting Code**. What is this code? Well, as also mentioned, companies use this in a number of Internet web browser systems right now! The purpose of this specific type of code is to correct errors that creep in when they transmit code. There are a number of possible causes for such errors occurring, such as poor transmission services, whether via wire, satellite, or whatever.

For example, if there is a solar eruption, the resulting radiation burst can interfere with satellites, and this can cause interference in transmissions, as well. Block Linear Code checks these transmissions against original versions sent and so corrects them when such errors creep in. Moreover, what is computer code? Well, it is nothing more than a set of instructions on how something should be done or run, as in possibly how a universe should be run, for example?

Additionally, if there is Block Linear Self Dual Error Correcting Code in the fundamental makeup of our universe, as there definitely seems to be, then it must be there for a good reason. In addition, even as with our code, there are going to be occasions when it doesn't work quite properly, or the correction itself, causes a "glitch" in the running of the program.

If Super String Theory does prove to be the correct basic theory of everything for our universe, then isn't it interesting we have correcting algorithms embedded in the very equations that describe our universe? This is exactly what any computer programmer would do in order to insure the stability of such a computer simulation! Moreover, nobody can come up with an alternate explanation of why it would be there.

**Conclusion:** The whole question of our universe being just information definitely has some real evidence to support the theory, including the ability to quantum teleport atoms, electrons, and photons by just sending their "information." This in itself argues powerfully for the idea of our universe just being information or mathematics.

Additionally, having binary code as part of the formulas that make up the theory of Super Symmetry, and not just any binary code at that, but code we have also designed specifically to be "self-correcting" for transmissions of data, adds to this idea of the universe as being just information/mathematics.

Added to this is, as well, is the idea that our universe "pixelates" or gets "grainy" on the small scale, becomes just particles, just as a computer game becomes just pixels on the small scale, is an incredible state of affairs. This is even more compelling when one considers that according to the above formula of the possibility of us just being a simulation, it is far more likely we are such a thing, rather than the real article.

Furthermore, if it is far more likely that our universe is a simulation, then this alters our perception of our universe and reality, and dramatically so.

Time, itself, then would truly be just an illusion, a manifestation or product of a running program of all our universe and us, and so easily altered, distorted, or traveled through by those "others" who created it all. In other words, time travel would be no barrier to the gamesters or originators of our simulation.

So are we just sentient characters in a vast simulation running for someone else's benefit? Are we really just a programmed simulation, perhaps one of many, and even maybe a program within a program, a "nested" one, as in the movie, *The Thirteenth Floor?*

If this is true, than what we see as time travel is just a built-in way, a mathematical "door," a convenient method for those "others" to move about within the parameters of their games or simulations. Time travel, then, is just another gaming device, as it were. Either time travelers could well be those who wish to experience the simulation directly or indirectly, or gamers who just wish to participate in a game, even as online gamers all participate in one grand game on the Internet, such as the *World of Warcraft, League of Legends,* or whatever.

If the idea seems incredible, then think again! In addition, this isn't about just a few "fringe" elements in science arguing for this sort of thing being so. We have mainstream and renowned scientists who are now raising this premise as an actual possibility, even as a probability.

Additionally, some of them are even stating that the odds are great of this being so, of us being some great computer simulation that is running, and again, perhaps one of countless other such simulations! Time travel then, is nothing compared to such an idea, and in fact, would almost have to be so, if only to allow those "others" to move about within the created simulations, to different eras of it.

To summarize, time travel may be real because it is nothing more than a tool, a simple gaming device. Nevertheless, is there any other evidence to support this idea, other than mathematical probabilities? Yes, there seems to be. We have touched on some of it here in this chapter, but now we will take a more in-depth look at such evidence of our universe being just a simulation.

Let's see if we can find any of those "glitches" in our reality. Furthermore, if they are there, what are the implications for time travel being real as a result?

# CHAPTER 16
# Glitches In Time—Synchronicities?

*"In Einstein's equation, time is a river. It speeds up, meanders, and slows down. The new wrinkle is that it can have whirlpools and fork into two rivers. So, if the river of time can be bent into a pretzel, create whirlpools and fork into two rivers, then time travel cannot be ruled out."*

—Michio Kaku

Here in this chapter, we will discuss two approaches to the idea of "time glitches." Time glitches are important in our discussion about time travel because they prove that time isn't nearly as "unalterable" as some might think. Even Einstein thought this with his idea that time was as a river with whirlpools, eddies, and currents in it. The two approaches to glitches are:

1. Individual/groups experiencing time glitches, and

2. Scientific evidence for the idea of time glitches being real.

Now again, just what is a time glitch? Well, it is anything out of the ordinary in the way time would flow, an error or inconsistency that is observable. The famous one from the movie, *The Matrix*, is where Keanu Reeves sees a cat walk by an open doorway twice in rapid succession.

He thinks it is a case of déjà vu, but his companions tell him it is a "glitch in the matrix," that is an observable discrepancy and when seen, it had implications…

So what are observable glitches in time? Well, starting with number one, the idea that individual and/or groups can experience time glitches, we have theories from the *Holographic Universe*, the bestselling book by now-deceased author, Michael Talbot. He observed and theorized that experiences of déjà vu actually could be a type of glitch in time, just as in the *Matrix* movie. Déjà vu, for those who aren't aware of it, is the feeling many sometimes get of having experienced something that has just happened before, and in the exact same way. Déjà vu is an unsettling feeling, but it is surprisingly common. So common are these phenomenon that they are even broken down into various types. Dr. Vernon M. Neppe in his 1983 book, titled, *The Psychology of Déjà Vu* states the following are the main types:

*déjà entendu,* which means, *already heard,*

*déjà éprouvé,* which means, *already tried or attempted,*

*déjà fait,* which means, *already done or accomplished,*

*déjà pensé* which means, *already thought or pondered,*

*déjà raconté,* which means, *already recounted or told,*

*déjà senti,* which means, *already felt,*

*déjà su,* which means, *already known (intellectually),*

*déjà trouvé,* which means, *already met,*

*déjà vécu,* which means, *already lived through or experienced,* and

*déjà voulu, which means, already wanted."*

Dr. Neppe even claims he has discovered many other types, as well, but these here are enough to illustrate just how common and how varied the whole idea of the déjà phenomenon is. Again, Michael Talbot felt these experiences could well be glitches in time.

Some scientists theorize this is not the case, and that it is just some sort of delayed response of the brain's neural responses in recognizing something, and so causing a sort of mental double take, a feedback loop. This, they claim, we then experience as déjà vu. However, as prosaic and practical an explanation as this might first appear, it has no scientific evidence to date to back it up all! None.

This so-called scientific theory to "explain" déjà vu, therefore, has no hard evidence of any sort to support the contention. Likewise, it doesn't explain the form of déjà vu where people can then state what is going to happen next and it does. This is the so-called paranormal form of déjà vu. Therefore, déjà vu, a phenomenon still totally unaccounted for, could actually be a form of a time glitch one can experience on a personal level. Even so, this is not the only such phenomenon of this type, and this fact is again, according to Michael Talbot. (For more information on Dr. Neppe's work, please see, *"References,"* at the end of this book.)

**Synchronicities.** Mr. Talbot in his *Holographic Universe* also went into depth about something called synchronicities. The famous psychiatrist, Carl Jung, who was a contemporary of Sigmund Freud, coined this term. A synchronicity, as defined by Carl Jung, is "a coincidence to meaningful to be ignored."

Of course, we all experience coincidences. They are common for many of us and we see them for what they are, just being mere coincidences. We even have some strange ones at times.

For instance, we may think of someone and then the phone immediately rings, and it is that person calling us. Yet, synchronicities are rarer than even these sorts of coincidences are, and often are even much harder to explain. There is also the element of time being involved in them for one thing. Synchronicities often seem to violate the normal laws of time as we see them.

Now again, as Carl Jung pointed out, and as did Michael Talbot, nobody is saying these aren't "coincidences." However, they are "coincidences to be so meaningful as not to be ignored," and according to Michael Talbot, they are the way the "universe sends us messages."

I've personally concluded the content of the synchronicity, in and of itself is not necessarily the message, but rather just the fact of the synchronicity having happened at all is. Here are just a few examples of personal synchronicities I've had. Compare them to your own, because almost all of us have had something like this happen to us:

I decided after decades to watch the old British *Avenger* TV series again, starring Dame Diana Rigg. I was watching an episode when a friend walked in. He inquired as to what I was looking at. I pointed out that this was once a very popular British TV series, and Diana Rigg, along with Patrick McNee, were exemplary in their parts.

We happened to be watching the very first episode where Diana Rigg was wearing her black leather suit, a rather cumbersome affair by today's standards, but cutting edge in the early 1960's for a woman to wear on TV. I pointed this fact out. My friend said he didn't much care for the outfit, being oddly bulky as it was.

The next day, less than 24 hours later, I watched the latest episode of *The Simpsons*. A British man robbed the local convenience store at gunpoint. By the way, he looked nothing like Patrick Macnee. There was also a woman in a black "cat" suit, who looked very like Diana Riggs. As they left the convenience store, the man referred to her as "Mrs. Peel," which is Diana Riggs' name in *The Avenger* series.

Just a coincidence? Yes, it is, most certainly, but one involving time. I had on a sudden whim to:

1. Decide to watch a TV show that was over fifty years old. Moreover, it was hard to find on my streaming network.

2. "Mrs. Peel" was in her type of costume and specifically singled out in a discussion with my friend. This was the first episode to portray her in such a costume.

3. A show created over fifty years later had a specific reference to it broadcast the next day, less than 24 hours later. Moreover, *The Simpsons* showed "Mrs. Peel" in that very same costume we had discussed. Furthermore, there could be no doubt, because her partner addressed her specifically as "Mrs. Peel." The sequence concerning this was no more than mere seconds in duration. Therefore, I could very easily have missed it. However, I didn't.

All these things had to come together for this synchronicity and obviously, there were many factors involved for this to happen. Definitely, this was a "coincidence to meaningful to be ignored." It was not only a result of my making two choices, first to watch the first show, and then the next one (which oddly, I usually don't watch anymore), but also the fact the one show was half a century old, while the other was brand new, and just airing for the first time. Ergo, items from two different times, decades apart, and a discussion about them signifying their significance, came together in a short space of time to create this synchronicity for my friend and me.

Nor is this the only synchronicity I've had. I, like countless others, have experienced many of them, so many in fact; I make it a point to mention them to others as backup proof of them having occurred, as they are occurring. Now, I've convinced my friend this is the case and that such things do happen and are real. He has no doubt they are taking place and by his own honest admission. Unfortunately, he can no more account for them, how they can happen, than I can, except the fact they do seem to transpire and frequently.

One more, and then I'll move on from this topic, and this was a MAJOR synchronicity. A number of years ago, I visited England and a friend there, staying with him for a couple of weeks. There was also another person there, as well, traveling with me.

Before going to England, I had just finished reading the *Da Vinci Code*. Intrigued by the contents, I read portions of the book aloud to my traveling companion, who had Dyslexia and so had difficulty reading. The portion I chose to read that day was about the subject of "rose lines," those ley lines that crisscross the world, and how special events and places occurred along them. This formed a big part of the concept of the book, the *Da Vinci Code*, by Dan Brown.

The book mentioned Rosslyn Chapel in Scotland, where Mary Magdalene's body might have been hidden at one time and that it was on such a "rose line" ("Rosslyn Chapel," a derivation of "rose line"). The book mentioned that further south along the rose line was famous Glastonbury Abbey and the even more famous Glastonbury Tor. I remarked after finishing the chapter that I'd like to go there on our trip to England, which we planned for just a week or so later. I had never been there before, so I wanted to see it.

That same afternoon, I received an email from my friend in England saying he thought it would be "cool" if we took a short trip of a few days to visit Glastonbury Abbey. He had never been there before either and so thought it might be fun and interesting.

This "coincidence" certainly surprised me. After all, not only had I just read the passage about this in the *Da Vinci Code* for the first time a mere few hours before, but then I had received an email saying we should go there, and this after I'd just expressed interest in going there, as well. Truly, this was a "significant" coincidence, and so a synchronicity.

In addition, all of this taking place in a few hours, but involving a book that had been published for some time, a location in England that had existed for hundreds of years, and then two sets of people, independently, deciding this would be a place to go to, makes this a synchronicity. Again, time seems to be a big factor in synchronicities.

It doesn't stop there! Upon arriving at my friend's home in England, we told him how weirdly timely his email had been, considering the circumstances, and that we felt it was a synchronicity. Our friend, being very British in an almost stereotypical way, was highly skeptical. He did not, nor does he even like to, believe in anything of such a "supernatural" or "highly suspect" nature. For him, it was just a random coincidence that I was making too much of.

In any case, we set out on our journey. We traveled northward. We stopped at a manor house, formerly the Lacock Abbey, where the first English photo took place in 1835. This was rather famous, because the picture taken from a window there may well be the oldest negative still surviving in England.

Naturally (as one does as a typical tourist), I took a picture from the same window, as well. From there, we then traveled on to Glastonbury Abbey and drank from the Sacred Water at the Chalice Well there. The water, as legend goes, is supposed to give one eternal life. (As a side note, if the water does impart this gift, it isn't in this world one receives it, because it seems everyone who imbibes it still eventually dies.)

From there, we traveled to nearby Glastonbury Tor and climbed the hill there to the tower. The place is famous as possibly being the site of not only the original King Arthur's Camelot (if it ever really existed), but also as the spot where Jesus, on his supposed travels with Joseph of Arimathea, who was a tin merchant, had landed in England, as mentioned in England's famous poem-cum-hymn, *Jerusalem*. Again, Jesus and Joseph of Arimathea were, according to oral tradition, said to have landed at Glastonbury Tor, which was then a high point in an area surrounded by a shallow sea (since drained and diked).

From there, we moved on to Wells Cathedral. After that, we headed further north, to a farmhouse we'd rented for a number of days on Lake Coniston in England's Lake District. Our English friend had handled the rental arrangements prior to our arrival in the United Kingdom. I was somewhat disappointed the place wasn't on the much more famous lake, Lake Windermere, but the farmhouse turned out to be wonderful.

While staying there, we journeyed even further north on a day trip. Seeing a sign off the main highway for a henge (England is riddled with such stone "henges," including the most famous, Stonehenge), we took a side-trip there. After that, we went on north and visited a portion of Hadrian's Wall, the one the Roman Emperor, Hadrian, had built across England to keep out the violent Scots of the day.

After that, we returned home, but on the way, we took a side-trip into Wales at my request, since we'd never made it to Wales before. We stopped at a village near Raglan Castle for lunch, and then went to the castle. From there we went home to my friend's house in Devon.

Why am I boring you with such a complete itinerary? Well, there is a very good reason, in fact, a startling one as we shall see, and it forms the most complete synchronicity I've ever experienced in my life. Upon arriving at my British friend's house in early evening, we were understandably tired after our busy trip. We went to our rooms to unpack.

Later, we came downstairs and the three of us sat in the front reception room to relax. My English friend turned on the television. It was precisely on the hour when he did so and without changing the channel, a documentary came on. This was just a couple of hours after us arriving at my friend's home. The documentary was about an Englishman who developed his own version of color photographic film. This was in the very early 20th Century. To prove its worth, he took his family in a huge touring car on a trip to take pictures using the film he'd invented.

Here is the truly strange part; his trip was not only identical to the one we'd just completed only hours before, but also in the exact order to the very same places! All of them! No less, but no more. He went to the abbey/manor house, the same as we. Next, he drove his family to the Glastonbury Abbey, then on to the Glastonbury Tor, and then Wells Cathedral. After that, he went on to the Lake District, where he stayed on Lake Coniston. This was just as we had done, and again, instead of the much more famous Lake Windermere.

The photographer then traveled north and stopped at the same "henge" we had, and photographed it, as well. He then moved on to Hadrian's Wall, and the same area of Hadrian's Wall, as well! (The wall, in total, is some 75 miles long...)

On his way home, he drove into Wales and stopped at the same village we had and then went on to Raglan Castle and took photos there, again, just as we had. This was incredible! Not only was this the same trip, in the same order, to the very same places, and there were plenty of others he could have gone to instead and in a different order, because England is just chock full of such places, but he had taken the trip just after the turn of the last century. This was almost 100 years before we took the very same trip!

Even so, stunned, we sat there and watched our journey unfold again, the one we'd just taken. This time, it was in the form of a series of ancient color photographs, but not really our own trip, but that of the photographer of old, and this just a mere few hours after completing our journey! Yes, I use many exclamation points here, but the incredible number of the coincidences involved was astounding to all three of us, not to mention the timing of them!

We were dead silent throughout the show. None of us spoke, not once, and none of us even seemingly dared to take a deep breath, as if in fear of drawing attention to ourselves, as we watched the TV documentary unfold. In short, we were speechless. At the end of it, our friend turned off the TV. A profound silence reigned, as we all just sat there.

I broke the quiet at last, by asking him:

*"Now do you see what we mean by synchronicities?"*

His response was a simple and terribly prosaic:

"*Yes, I do.*"

That was it. This answer didn't satisfy me, of course, and it wasn't nearly enough in my estimation, considering what had just happened, what we had just witnessed.

"*Well?*" I persisted. "*What do you think about it all?*" I mean, the man must have thought something after just witnessing all of that!

"*I don't,*" he said. "*I don't want to think about it, or want to talk about it.*" Moreover, he didn't. Although we are still friends to this day, many years later, we have NEVER discussed this profound synchronicity again. My friend won't touch the subject, no more than he would touch the third rail of an electrified train track.

His answer to the event seems to have been strictly to pretend it never happened, to ignore it utterly, although he does admit that it did occur. Then, we all deal with the incredible in our own ways…and for some; it's by a blanket denial of them. Oh, again, he doesn't deny this inconceivable synchronicity occurred. He just refuses to dwell upon the implications of the event in any way, or to discuss them with me. It just happened and that was that, it seems, at least, as far as he was concerned.

For the life of me, I can't remember the photographer's name in the documentary, and neither can the others, but that we saw the show is not in doubt. That is the crux of our incredible synchronicity. That we saw almost century-old photographs of our exact trip and in the same order, we had taken it, and only hours after completing the journey ourselves, is also not in doubt.

Again, the time factor enters here. It wasn't just that we saw the ancient photographs of our journey on a TV show, but that we turned it on, quite by accident and at random, at the exact time and on the very channel the show came on, and within hours of having completed our own travels. The coming together of these three events and so precisely is truly amazing.

Synchronicities for me seem to have to come together in short spans of time, usually no more than 24 hours, or so for their adjacent "parts" at most. After all, to take that trip and then see the documentary years later wouldn't be nearly so telling an event as seeing it after just having arrived home from the trip! Even so, it would still classify as a very strange coincidence even with such a delay, I think, or rather series of coincidences.

Again, an amazing set of coincidences by anyone's standards, one should think and very meaningful ones. This then, is how synchronicities seem to work. A series of events take place in *different times,* and then somehow all come together to create one of these weird sets of coincidences at a critical moment, when their significance is higher than it would normally be.

The strange thing is that time, as a restricting factor, doesn't enter into it at all. Time doesn't seem to matter, or somehow something circumvents its limitations in some way. Yet at the same time, the timing element is an integral and intense part of the synchronicity itself. The events have to occur close together to be meaningful to the observer or participant (victim?) If this is so, then it also shows time is not the static thing we might think it to be.

There have been many more synchronicities in my life. Some of these have been large ones, and some smaller, but all stun me. Moreover, in most cases, I'm not alone. Others are somehow involved and, thankfully, can attest they are real.

This is important for me, since to experience them solely on my own, without any sort of proof in the form of witnesses, would be intensely frustrating for me, as one can readily imagine. Synchronicities also seem to come in clusters, and as with this one. However, never have I had such an amazing one as on that one trip to England.

How is something like this even possible, a synchronicity that spans decades if not a full century in order to work and the coincidences coming so thick and fast, in so many aspects/details that are not just alike, but identical? I have no idea how this can be, but it does seem to illustrate how time is either very fluid in such matters of synchronicities, or perhaps time is truly an illusion after all?

One might also ask why it happened to the three of us. I have no answer, except to say these do happen many times for me, and even recently, but again, not on this scale! Nor am I alone. Others report this to me, as well.

If, as Michael Talbot in *The Holographic Universe* says, synchronicities happen to many of us, and once noticed, seem to happen more often, he seems to be right. Furthermore, if they are a "message from the universe," I have no idea what the message is, other than it is to say that there is, as Shakespeare put it in his play, *Hamlet*:

*"There are more things in heaven and earth, Horatio, than are dreamt of in your philosophy."*

Indeed, there does seem to be. In addition, the fluidity of time, as Einstein explained, seems to be one of them.

**Conclusion:** The point here is that glitches in time, such as déjà vu and synchronicities, are a phenomenon that does seem to exist and is real. Synchronicities seem to gather events from different times and somehow bring them together at precise and crucial moments to create powerful and meaningful effects. Their exact meaning, their cause, is something yet to be determined, but that they exist, seems to be little in doubt. One can call them super coincidences, just coincidences in a series, or whatever, but they do happen.

Not only do most of us get the occasional feelings of déjà vu, but so many of us have synchronicities that a famous psychologist invented a term for them, and a major New York Times' bestseller, *The Holographic Universe*, wrote about them and in depth. Those aren't the only books on the subject. Check out Amazon or peruse the bookshelves at your local bookstores. They are loaded with books on the subject of synchronicities.

Have you had synchronicities? If not, now that you are aware of them, there is a good chance you will. Oddly, this is how it usually works, and even as Michael Talbot said. It is almost as if when we take notice of the universe, it then seems to "notice" us back. Additionally, these "glitches" in our reality, synchronicities, just couldn't exist without the weird time factors involved, or rather the distortion of time, as we know it. In fact, in a way, synchronicities almost seem to form a kind of time travel, or at least seem to sidestep it somehow, for they bring things together that just shouldn't happen when and how they do.

**Are Synchronicities A Subjective Form Of Evidence?** Most definitely, they are. I agree with this assessment. Even with witnesses to such "meaningful coincidences," critics can still argue they are just that after all, mere coincidences. Granted, in the case of the one above, they are truly incredible sets of coincidences!

Still, it is again important to point out that nobody is arguing against this part of it, of synchronicities being coincidences. It is even a part of Carl Jung's principle definition of them. The only thing people like Carl Jung and Michael Talbot are saying, and I'm saying as well in this case, is that sometimes they are incredibly meaningful and very strange, indeed. Moreover, they seem to defy logic and time! They are truly glitches in our reality and universe on some level, it seems.

For the three of us involved in the Glastonbury trip, we have no doubt that something truly bizarre took place. Moreover, this strange happening intimately wrapped itself up with time, and even implied a form of time travel, in that time itself was no barrier for the synchronicities to take place. Two of us are willing to discuss the events and have, repeatedly, trying to make sense of it all. The third, again, readily acknowledges the actual occurrence of the event, but for his private reasons, has never discussed it with me again. If he has with others, I have no idea...

Furthermore, in his book, Michael Talbot provided much more additional evidence for glitches in reality than I've provided here. This evidence is for not only synchronicities, but other strange matters, as well, including people seeing visions from the past, as with the two ladies who went to Versailles. *The Holographic Universe* makes for some powerful and very convincing reading with its ideas about all of this. I highly recommend the book.

However, if one desires a more concrete form of evidence of time glitches, there is some of that, as well. In the next chapter, we shall see experiments that seem to prove that time is not the manifestly unsurpassable barrier we always once thought it to be, and certainly not with regard to human consciousness.

# CHAPTER 17
# More Glitches — Human Consciousness And Time

*"When we see the shadow on our images, are we seeing the time 11 minutes ago on Mars? Or are we seeing the time on Mars as observed from Earth now? It's like time travel problems in science fiction. When is now; when was then?"*

—Bill Nye

The quotation above is a very interesting one. It raises all sorts of issues, and ones that Einstein himself raised, as well. For instance, just what is "the present?" What does it include? One of the things pointed out with this problem of what time we are in, what "present," is straightforward. For example:

An astronomer in our time right now looks through a telescope (we'll pretend the telescope can see a very long ways and clearly). He sees another world like Earth, and on that planet, he sees an alien astronomer gazing back up at him. Now, if that alien astronomer is a long ways a way, the farther he is, the further back in time our human astronomer is seeing him, because light takes time to travel from there to here and from here to there.

So if the alien astronomer and his planet is, say, 1,000 light years away, and our astronomer is gazing up at him that means our human astronomer is seeing 1,000 years into the past of that planet. He is seeing an alien astronomer on that planet that lived 1,000 years ago. Yet, our human astronomer is seeing him right now! Therefore, his view of the alien is part of his human "present," although it is 1,000 years in the past for the alien, who by our "present" time would be long dead.

Now let's do the reverse. The alien astronomer is looking up at the Earth, as we mentioned, but he sees the Earth as it was 1,000 years ago from his time. He does not see our human astronomer here on Earth, because for the alien, our human astronomer is in his world's distant future. Even so, the alien's view of Earth during the period of the very early Medieval Period for Europe is part of the alien's "present." He is alive and seeing it right then.

So whose present in this case is the real one? Is it the alien's with his view of Earth as it was long ago, and our current present then still being 1,000 years in his future? Alternatively, is it our "present" with the view of an alien that lived 1,000 years ago incorporated into it? In truth, it is both simultaneously, which is a hard thing to grasp and understand.

If one extend that light cone from both planets (light travels outward from a source in a cone shape like a flashlight beam, hence the term "light cone"), to where they intersect, you have a sort of see-saw arrangement. You have two beings on two different worlds looking toward each other at two very different times, but creating a sort of mixed present of the two, as a result.

Again, rather confusing, but that is our whole point here. Just what constitutes the present is rather up for grabs, it seems. We think we have a handle on it, but just look through a telescope and all bets are off. Even Mars, as in the quotation at the beginning of this chapter comments on, falls into this category for us, because there is an eleven-minute time distance (on average) between the time that our light leaves the Earth and strikes Mars, and vice versa. Hence, we have the problems of the quotation above. When we look through a telescope at Mars, on the one hand, we are seeing it as it was eleven minutes ago, but at the same time, the way we are seeing it now, is a part of our "now," our present. Therefore, the present seems to be a very malleable and fluid sort of thing.

**Consciousness seems to exist outside of time.** Moreover, the quotation at the beginning of this chapter above is an incredible statement in another way, but one that seems true enough, as well. This is according to multiple studies at universities done on the subject. In addition, the results seem to be that the present is…well…again, very subjective.

At this point, we again come to the murky world of what is reality and what is consciousness, and how they seem to be colliding with each other in science and in time, itself. Some even go so far as to say reality is entirely a result of consciousness. For instance, as seen on *Through The Wormhole*, the television series starring Morgan Freeman, repeated experiments at different universities have led to an unsettling conclusion about the human mind and time.

One study clearly showed a very strange phenomenon. The study, titled, *"Predictive Physiological Anticipation Preceding Seemingly Unpredictable Stimuli: A Meta-Analysis"* clearly demonstrated results that showed the body responded to certain types of events before the events had actually occurred.

The conclusion of this and similar studies is simple, yet profound. It appears the human consciousness exists in not only the here and now, the exact present, but also slightly in the past, as well as slightly into the future. As described by some researchers, there seems to be a definite "overlap" of time in this regard when it comes to the human consciousness. In fact, experiments have shown that humans seem to be capable of "seeing" into the future. (Again, according to *Through The Wormhole* and other sources. Please see links under *"References"* at end of book.)

**The Mind Can See the Future.** The ability to see future events, or at least "feel" dangerous things impending, is approximately two to ten seconds in length, or on average, about five seconds before they actually happen. As Morgan Freeman explained on his show, this might have evolved as a beneficial survival factor for humans. If one has a few seconds of warning, mentally, of something dangerous impending, one has more time to react and change the outcome. His example was of someone driving down a highway, approaching an intersection, and suddenly getting the feeling something bad was going to happen there. Five seconds is just enough time to slow down to avoid the coming collision.

Of course, people often dismiss such feelings as these out of hand, as evidenced by the number of accidents that do happen anyway. Moreover, the intuitive feeling could well be more pronounced in some of us versus others, and better developed, as well. Researchers need further tests to determine if this is true or not. These tests were simple. Scientists wired subjects to GSR (Galvanic Skin Response) machines to show their bodies' physical responses to a series of random images shown to them.

The pictures were like a slide show, with pleasant images shown and again quite randomly, but with an occasional (also randomly) horrific image included every so often.

The participants in the experiment, both the testers and those tested, had no idea when such images would appear, so there could be no way of telegraphing the coming pictures to the participants, either overtly, or covertly, and thus possibly contaminating the test results.

When shown the images, researchers discovered that in a large number of subjects, their bodies reacted to the horrific image *before it actually appeared!* This would occur about two to ten seconds before the event. Consequently, the responses were five seconds on average, before the subjects saw the picture. The body functions showed marked changes, as if in anticipation of what was about to come. These changes did not occur with pleasant images, but only the shocking ones.

Upon publishing the first results, the researchers themselves made it clear there might be errors they could not ascertain in the experiment, perhaps some problem in the way they gathered the data electronically that might account for this two-to-ten-second discrepancy. They actively encouraged other researchers to comb through their tests results and methods to see if they could find flaws in them.

Other researchers could not determine there were any flaws in the way the experiments had proceeded, but even so, at several universities, they repeated the experiments and with some refinements to make doubly sure of the results.

The outcomes were the same. The ability for the human body to react before something actually occurred was a significant and unexplainable response. That is, the response was unexplainable if one didn't think the human consciousness could "feel" coming events that would occur two, to up to ten seconds or so, into the future.

**The Mind Lives In The Past**. We have also mentioned the human consciousness exists slightly in the past. This is because other studies have shown there is a tiny delay before images of what one has seen striking the retina of their eye can then travel up the optic nerve as neural signals to the brain. This takes about one-tenth of a second to complete. Researchers call this delay "neural lag." This means the brain gets the image one is seeing through their eyes, but with a one-tenth of a second delay. In short, our brain is always seeing what has occurred one-tenth of a second in the past and must function using that delayed imagery as if it were seeing the actual present.

Such studies have indicated people; although they are actually getting this delayed image of an occurrence, still respond as if there was no delay time at all. How can the human brain do this? After all, the human mind has a problem. It must work with input slightly from the past because of this delay, and so it somehow must then compensate for this fact and still function as if it were in the immediate present. Again, how?

Well, once more, the mind seems to somehow be able to travel through time, or at least, exist slightly out of phase with time, if only minutely, in this respect.

The mind seems to adjust for the delay in any stimulus the brain receives and the fact it thus lives one-tenth of a second in the past by acting as if it simply doesn't. This is a strange thing to comprehend, but apparently true. Moreover, there is no doubt this neural lag exists, because it is easily measured and has been repeatedly by different groups of researchers to confirm the findings.

Somehow, the human brain has learned to compensate for this time lag, has managed to develop a way to offset for the time delay. The brain seems to create its own version of a present reality it doesn't really have access to, and so use a sort of predictive ability to know what will be occurring just one-tenth of a second into the future to compensate for the lag time it incurs. One might think this is not a big deal, a mere tenth of a second, but it is!

Think about a baseball or football player catching a ball, for instance, or a racer driving a fast car, or any type of action that requires an "instant response." Our brains manage to tell us how to do these things, even though a tenth of a second is a long time for a fastball, one that may be traveling as much as 90 miles an hour.

Yet, the player is still be able to intercept the ball (if catching it), despite the fact it has traveled many feet more since he last actually "saw" the ball. The ball during the lag time has already moved farther than the player is actually able to see at the needed instant, since the player is always one-tenth of a second behind in his vision of the thing.

The same thing occurs with racecar drivers. Even at just 60 miles per hour, the car will have already moved 8.8 feet farther in just one-tenth of a second. The faster the racecar driver goes the greater the distance traveled in one-tenth of a second.

Double the speed and the distance increases significantly. Triple the speed and the distance becomes truly a big factor and racecar drivers often go at or near such high speeds.

So how does the human mind compensate for the fact it is always one-tenth of a second behind, always exists, for practical purposes, one-tenth of a second in the past? How does it manage to allow the driver to make turns in time, to stop in time when traveling at considerable speeds? This answer is unknown. Yet despite our ignorance of how we do it, we can do it. This is incredible that we can still function so well this way, and despite this lag time with our minds living always in a moment that has already passed.

Does it ever cause us problems? Possibly. One scientist claims that one type of optical illusion or even more types might just be the result of the brain trying to predict the future and finding its prediction is not in correspondence with the reality of a tenth of a second later. Hence, we have optical illusions created.

In short, our brains are constructing an up-to-date, "present" reality from delayed information by accurately managing to predict the future. One can see how this wouldn't be a real problem if something is moving slowly, but again, a car, jet, train, or whatever traveling at high speeds would seem to be a whole other matter.

**Conclusion:** What does all this mean for time travel? Well, apparently, and according to repeated scientific experiments under controlled conditions, the human consciousness is capable of traveling a short distance into the future, two to ten seconds. This is especially so with regard to impending dangers and so might just be a form of an evolutionary advantage that has developed in us to help with our survival.

Furthermore, scientific studies have also confirmed the idea of "neural lag," the fact that being a physical body; humans are subject to the laws of physics.

Therefore, it takes "time" for a neural signal to get from our ears, eyes, nose, mouth, or sense of touch to our brains. Our brain and one would then assume our consciousness, as well, has to live slightly in the past, about one-tenth of a second at all times.

Yet, somehow, our conscious minds compensate for living in the past by being able to predict what is going on in the present, the "real right now." Otherwise, we wouldn't be to do all the things we do. Again, how this is possible, scientists are not certain. They only have theories. Still, the fact this is so is not in doubt.

The conclusion of all this is simple; the human mind, the consciousness seems to be able to, if not actually travel through time, still be able to predict events to come, if only on a very short time span. Once more, how can it do this, how can our minds know the future at all, unless it somehow has access to some limited degree to the future?

Furthermore, we can't really pin down what is "the present?" What is our present is someone else's future or past, and vice versa. Although we may see something through a telescope in the present, we are really looking into someone else's past. When we look at other people or things, we are actually always seeing them how they were a tenth of a second ago.

So what is time to the human consciousness? Well, it is not a solid "real" thing, apparently. Time is far more subjective than we might have thought possible just a few decades ago. Furthermore, time travel, if only in the form of the human mind, seems to be a reality.

Again, time, it seems, is far more fluid and malleable than we once ever conceived and it may be that time as we think of it, as a fixed clock ticking away the seconds, doesn't really exist at all. Repeatedly now, we seem to keep coming to this same conclusion through different means.

# CHAPTER 18
# Quantum Physics And Time Travel

*"... [You] can think of time travel, the process of going from the future into the past, as a kind of teleportation of information from now to back then. Moreover, we were actually able to use a simple quantum computer to demonstrate this effect."*

—**Seth Lloyd, *A Quantum Leap in Computing***

Now we come to that most dreaded but necessary of subjects with regard to time, and that is quantum mechanics, also known as quantum physics. Why is it important? Well, this is because quantum physics and time seem to be intricately involved in many ways, so much so that one can't really discuss many aspects of quantum physics without also discussing time or perhaps, the total lack of time as we know it, if in truth time exists at all on the quantum level.

Therefore, there needs to be some information about the subject here in this book. However, as promised, there won't be any sort of mathematics involved.

Again, the purpose of this book is not to bury the reader under formulas that only an advanced mathematician would understand in any case, but rather to give a simple overview of the subject, because it is just so important to time travel. Even the definition of quantum mechanics/quantum physics, despite the rather formidable title, is really an easy one:

**Quantum physics is merely the study and the attempt to understand the nature of that which is very small, meaning atoms or "subatomic" (smaller than atoms) particles that help to make up atoms.** That's it. That's all there is to it, sort of...

As mentioned, we all live in the "macroscopic world." This is the world of big things, like trees, rocks, people, animals, stars, planets, galaxies, etc. These all seem to behave according to certain and ever increasingly well-defined sets of rules that we know simply as "the laws of physic," or otherwise knowns as "classic physics." These are the rules of nature we all more or less know and live by.

Yet, on the quantum level, the level of the incredibly small, such as those atoms we mentioned, or the electrons, proton, neutrons and other tiny particles that make up those larger atoms, things get very weird, indeed. They get so weird, in fact, that we have to use a completely different set of mathematical rules to describe them. We call those rules quantum physics.

Why is this necessary? Well, it seems that nothing on the incredibly small level behaves in what we would consider reasonable or even rational ways. Subatomic particles don't conform to the "laws of physics" of our bigger world at all, not in the least.

The first thing to know is that subatomic particles, although often shown in this way, DO NOT behave like colliding billiard balls, for instance. Far from it. Moreover, the fact that quantum mechanics is weird and hard to comprehend because of this is not in dispute by anyone. Even one of the original pioneers of this field, the Nobel Prize winning physicist, Niels Bohr, stated:

*"If anybody says he can think about quantum physics without getting giddy, that only shows he has not understood the first thing about them."*

That sums up the nature of this subject, so again, we will not try to go into depth on all the aspects of quantum physics. Just remember that we have one set of physics for the macroscopic, things on our scale as it were, and a completely different set for the world of subatomic particles. Moreover, neither sets of these mathematical rules works for the other. They do not cross over, or at least, we always thought this to be so, until recently...

Rather than attempt to try to understand most of this subject, a task better left to quantum physicists and their books, we will concentrate on the time aspects of quantum physics. We will delve into what it tells us about time, and how time behaves in the world of the very small.

Trust me; time does NOT behave as it does in our world of normal-sized objects. Again, the implications for quantum physics and time are incredible. As the author, Richard K. Morgan, said:

*"In the future, maybe quantum mechanics will teach us something equally chilling about exactly how we exist from moment to moment of what we like to think of as time."*

Why all this excitement about how time behaves for very small particles? Well, because:

**1.** Those tiny subatomic particles help make up atoms, and

**2.** Those atoms then go on to make up not only us, but also everything we see on our scale in the universe. Therefore, not only planets, but also the stars, galaxies, and even we are the sum total of quantum particles and therefore, those particles could well have a direct bearing on time and even the possibility of time travel for us, or even if time is "real" at all as we think of it.

For example, is the fact the human consciousness seems to "float" in time, being partly in the past and able to "feel" impending dangers up to ten seconds into the future a manifestation or side effect of quantum time behavior? This could well be the case, because again, and this can't be overstressed, particles on the quantum level do not behave like things at our level of existence. For instance:

**1. Particles behave differently when observed than when not observed.** This is an incredible phenomenon, but one well proven. It means when we are observing a particle, it behaves in one way, and when we aren't observing it, the thing behaves differently. Again, this is not like billiard balls would behave. What causes this difference? Nobody is sure, but it has given rise to all sorts of theories about reality, as we perceive it.

**2. Subatomic matter has a "particle-wave duality."** This may sound hard to understand but the reality of this concept is very simple, if still incredible. It's the understanding of *why and how* subatomic particles can behave this way that is much harder to comprehend and confounds every quantum physicist on the planet.

Why is this so? Well, particles on the subatomic scale act as if solid particles when observed, like those billiard balls to which I keep referring. When not observed, however, the particles act just like waves. This is a simplification of the idea somewhat, but it is very close to the mark.

An example of this is if we think of a particle as an item, such as a plastic bottle we might seal and throw into the sea in the hopes it drifts with the currents to another place far across the ocean, eventually for someone else "over there" to find.

However, where the bottle remains a bottle throughout this process in our macroscopic world, bobbing along in the water with the currents, a particle in the subatomic world would turn into a wave. This wave would emanate out in all directions and wherever that wave first hit land, the particle would pop into existence as a particle again, or that plastic bottle, to use our analogy.

In other words, our bottle would turn into a wave with just a "probability" of hitting any particular landmass first. It would spread out as a wave and only become a bottle again when it first hit land somewhere. The weird part is once the wave-like particle does this, all the rest of the wave disappears instantaneously.

The particle is a particle again in just the one place and no other. Moreover, while traveling across the sea, to continue the analogy, our bottle only remains as a wave when not observed. If we trained our vision on it, it would instantly become a bottle again while we were looking at it! Again, this is very weird behavior by "normal" circumstances.

Even weirder is this happens whenever someone observes the particle. When not being observed, it acts as a wave. When observed, it becomes a particle, or as physicists put it, the particle wave undergoes a collapsing wave function and so becomes a particle again.

This idea also applies with regard to how electrons can go from one "state" to another without passing through any points in between. I'm sure you have heard the term before, a "quantum leap," where a particle jumps from point "A" to point "C" without ever having physically to pass through point "C."

Accordingly, an electron does not act like a train crossing over land, traveling through city after city to get to its final destination.

Instead, an electron can "quantum leap" from one level ("state") to another. Again, to use the analogy here, they could pop from one city to a far city without ever having had to pass through any cities in between. Again, this is a simple analogy, but it works well to describe this phenomenon.

3. **Non-local nature of particles.** This is another bizarre feature of the quantum world. When the Large Hadron Collider at CERN, Switzerland, creates pairs of particles, they can become "quantum entangled." This means that one cannot describe them separately, but instead one has to describe them only as a whole, or a pair.

This "pairing" can include a number of features or characteristics of the particles in question, including their momentum, spin, and more. We aren't concerned here with what these terms mean, but rather merely the fact the particles have these properties.

What is important is that if you change something in one particle, the spin for instance, the other one must change its spin accordingly. This is so, even if the particles aren't together, and are widely separated. Yet, it is as if somehow, one particle "knows" what has happened to the other one, without being in direct contact with it. Moreover, *this "knowing" appears to happen instantaneously!*

This holds true whether only a meter, one hundred meters, or even thousands, millions, and billions of light years separate the particles! The one particle will instantly somehow "know" the other particle has altered its properties, and so will change accordingly.

This boggles the mind, because it means that somehow, the particles are in some way sending the necessary information to each other and *the speed of light, that basic speed law and major constant of the universe, is not a barrier!*

The implications of this fact are fantastic! It seems to show that time for these "non-local" particles (since their behavior acts anywhere and everywhere, and not just "locally") doesn't exist! The particles seem to be able somehow to function without any sort of constraints with regard to the fundamentals, the very laws of time, as we know them.

It would be as if twin brothers or sisters could talk to each other, instantly, whether one was on the other side of the room or on the other side of the universe. An amazing thing to consider, is it not?

That this all seems inconceivable is obvious not only to us, but again, to every physicist who works in the quantum field. However, up until recently, we thought this didn't have an effect on our world of bigger things, the "macro world." So although matter at the subatomic level might behave as if time doesn't matter, at our level, things are different, and behave much more logically and rationally, or so we thought until recently…

**Weird Quantum Effects On The Visible Scale.** As mentioned, up until now, physicists thought the two worlds, ours, the one of large things like ourselves, and the other, the world of the very small were separate. It was as if there was a natural barrier between them. Our world ran by the "normal" laws of physics, while the world of the very tiny ran by the laws of quantum physics, and "never the twain shall meet." Well, it seems scientists now fear this may have been a big: "WHOOPS!" Why do I say this? Well, because scientists have discovered that the weird world of quantum effects can apparently cross over into our world.

In California, some researchers have observed weird quantum effects on an object big enough to consider as being "macroscopic," or on our scale. This means the thing was big enough to see with the unaided eye, so it was hardly microscopic, let alone on the very tiny scale of the quantum world.

This means the barrier between the two worlds doesn't have nicely set boundaries like those that we once thought. By the way, this is a new discovery, and it has shaken the world of physics both classical, and quantum alike.

The problem arises from a property of things on the tiny quantum scale. Particles can exist in two states simultaneously and this seems no problem for them. This double state of existence is as if one state of a particle superimposes itself over another, and so scientists call it "superposition."

This fundamental superposition property of the very small is on the quantum level, with atom-sized structures, and even with regard to a carbon molecule, a so-called buckyball (named for the famous Buckminster Fuller of geodesic arrangements, which a "buckyball" resembles) showing this behavior.

That molecule, however, is only composed of 60 atoms, and so is still well down into the quantum world level. So again, quantum effects seemed safely limited to the truly microscopic, because we had not seen them manifest in larger objects than this molecule.

Nevertheless, one reason we might not have noticed it on larger levels is that effects of nature help mask quantum effects, apparently. Heat causes atoms to vibrate for instance and so can camouflage what would otherwise be observable quantum effects because of this vibration.

Nonetheless, if one cools the object down to near absolute zero, one can observe quantum effects in atoms. Again, we're still talking on the extremely small scale, though. The problem has always been to try to get larger objects cold enough to do this, to show evidence of quantum effects where there isn't exterior interference, which could hide them.

**A Quantum Drum.** This whole situation changed with a stunning breakthrough at the University of California in Santa Barbara. Researcher Andrew Cleland, along with others there, came up with the idea of a mechanical resonator, one made of aluminum nitride. The good thing about such a resonator made of this material is it is something like a tuning fork, and one that works well when cooled to near absolute zero.

They did much more besides this, as well, to make this work, but the point here is, once they created the "quantum drum," it worked for its purposes and worked well! Big enough to see with the human eye, the quantum drum was composed of nearly a trillion atoms and not just sixty as with the buckyball molecule. The quantum drum formed a disc, or very thin type of drumhead.

When they electrically measured the quantum drum by using a "quantum thermometer," they found an incredible thing. They were able to create, simultaneously, "excitation" in the quantum drum, as well as at the same time making it have no excitation in it at all! What does this mean? Well, something we can see with the naked eye manifested "superposition," thus being in two separate states at the very same time!

Again, this superposition effect was once thought to exist only on the quantum level, but it now seems it exists on our level, the macroscopic one, as well. Something in "our world" of the very large can exist in two distinctly different states at once!

How can this possibly be? What are the repercussions for us, especially us, as individuals? If superposition can exist for us, and we can be in two states at once, is this the explanation, for example, for how our minds can exist not only in the here and now, but also in the close past, and near future, as well?

Is this what makes it possible for the human consciousness to straddle time, so to time travel? This discovery might well have such implications and far-reaching ones at that.

For example, on the quantum level, an electron can be in two places at once. If quantum effects of the same type can occur on our scale of the universe, can the same be true of solid objects in the "normal" world, including ourselves? Can we exist in two places at once? Moreover, if so, would this be into parallel realities? For a more detailed explanation about this discovery, please see the link to the article at *Physics World* under *"References."*

One thing is certain about all this, it means things might be possible in our reality that until now we thought were impossible, or almost impossible. If time, as some physicists say, doesn't really exist on the quantum scale, might that be true for our scale, as well? Are we laboring under the false assumption that time is real when it is not? Is time as we know it just an illusion?

If so, then time travel for us is a distinct possibility, a very real one, because there would be no "real" barrier to this happening. Moreover, communications, the sending and receiving of information might be possible in an instantaneous way, whereas now we are subject to the limitations of the speed of light, thus the reason for the lag when one reporter talks to another on television and they two are widely separated. We've all watched as an anchor person asks a question and the reporter in the field just stands there nodding his head in silence until he receives the message and so can then respond

So even here on Earth, we experience the limitations of the speed of light in such things. It just takes time for messages to go from the ground up to a satellite, and then sent to another one, downloaded, received, and then sent back again. Of course, there is the processing time involved for our equipment there, as well, that must be included in this lag, but the speed of light is a real restriction in how quickly we can send and receive information.

**Conclusion:**

*"The multiverse is no longer a model, it is a consequence of our models."*

Physicist, Aurelien Barrau, of CERN made this statement. A multiverse implies exactly what it says, more than one universe, and not just more than one, but a number of them so large, we probably cannot truly conceive of just how many universes might make up the "multiverse," of if there is any limit to that number at all. There well could be an infinity of universes within the multiverse.

This means, that if such parallel universes exist in their multitudes, it is entirely possible there are ones so like our own as to be hard for anyone to distinguish the difference.

That is, except of course, if someone's loved ones or personal lives are affected, or their memories are of things that did happen, but just not in this particular universe they may have accidentally somehow stumbled into. Therefore, the idea of crossing over to parallel timelines just isn't as weird as we might think. In fact, it might just be entirely possible, and as the one earlier quotation implied, be happening all the time and most of us just don't realize it, because the changes from one universe to the next are too small to notice.

Moreover, the Large Hadron Collider has come across some other strange things, as well. Some particles seem to "disappear" as one scientist put it, for incredibly brief but real periods. Some argue that these disappearances are because the particles are traveling briefly to other dimensions/universes. Some physicists even argue that gravity, a very weak force overall compared to the other forces of nature, is either "leaking" into our universe or might even be "leaking out" into other dimensions, thus making it seem weaker than it otherwise would be.

As we have seen in this chapter, the universe is a very strange place. What we think of as solid and "real" on our scale is hardly the case on the atomic/subatomic level. There, particles can exist in more than one place at one time. Particles are "non-local" in that they seem to be able to interact with each other at a distance instantaneously, as if ignoring the limitation of that supposedly universal law, the speed of light.

Furthermore, just recently we now have found real evidence some of this quantum weirdness, at least, can exist on our level, the large level. Objects we can see with the naked eye can have superposition; exist in two simultaneous states at once. This must mean, by extrapolation, that time isn't working as we thought it would for such objects on our scale either, that they must have at least some "non-local" attributes to them, as well. Does that mean that we, too, have this same attribute?

If so, what does this mean for us? Well, for one thing, it means the once safe world of ours, the one we think of as reality, as being solid and well ordered, just isn't so at all. Quantum weirdness is leaking through. In addition, if it can leak through to objects we can see, then that means it probably can affect us, personally, as well. It is entirely conceivable then, that we may be subject to "non-local" behavior when it comes to time, as well. We might then be the victims of sudden transpositions in time, forward or backward. Perhaps, it might also account for us being able to see events in future times, or out of the past. We might even switch to another reality or parallel world, as some scientists think particles might be able to do.

In other words, our world is not the steadfast reality we think it is, but it has kinks and cracks in it, things from the quantum world affecting it directly. Again, with superposition, this now is a proven fact, and simply is not in doubt anymore.

Therefore, time as we know it, or think we know it, may not exist. It may truly be a sort of illusion, or something fundamentally different from what we think of it as. If this is so, then time travel is a distinct possibility, since it would violate no laws of the quantum reality that might be directly affecting our so-called concept of a stable reality. Do we have more evidence of such possible kinks and cracks in the universe? Yes, we do, as we will see in the following chapter.

# CHAPTER 19

# Cracks In The Universe

*"Man ... can go up against gravitation in a balloon, and why should he not hope that ultimately he may be able to stop or accelerate his drift along the Time-Dimension, or even turn about and travel the other way."*

— H.G. WELLS, *The Time Machine*

As mentioned in the last chapter, our universe may have problems; there may be cracks in it on the quantum level. These cracks might cause, through their interactions with so-called "dark matter" to cause even stars to "tremble." Yes, something can cause even stars to shake and shiver, as with star quakes! As strange as that is, one might well ask what does this have to do with time travel. Well, we will get to that very shortly.

Our GPS network of satellites that keep extremely accurate time with their atomic clocks might be able to do more than just help us to locate where on a map we might be. They might also help us to learn much more about the nature of dark matter and even support a new theory.

Of course, one then wonders, just what is dark matter? Well, despite the name, scientists know very little about it, almost nothing of its nature, in fact. Then, that doesn't seem to stop them from naming the stuff, even so, as if by naming it, they then know what it is.

Again, they don't. They have, at this point, only a vague idea, one that might or might not be correct. Despite this, they have been able to learn some things about the properties of dark matter. There are various estimates of just how much of the matter in the universe may be composed of dark matter, but the most common figure seems to be just about 80%. If this is so, then that means the vast majority of our universe is unseen and completely unknown by scientists and us.

In other words, all our theories about the nature of our universe, how it formed, etc., are all founded on just a tiny fraction of the evidence currently available to us, with the vast majority of the universe (and so the biggest part of the evidence, accordingly), being dark matter and dark energy, as well, not even being included. Obviously, this means we have a very big, big hole in the understanding of the form and perhaps the origin of our universe! This also includes our concepts of how time might function, as well and this is where time travel begins to come into it.

However, this doesn't mean scientists aren't trying to learn about dark matter. For instance, Andrei Derevianko of the Univeristy of Nevada, as well as others, have come up with a theory that there might be faults or "kinks" running throughout the universe. These kinks would be on the quantum level, and run through quantum fields like cracks or fissures in the makeup of the universe.

What does this actually imply? Well, for starters, it would mean that subatomic particles, those particles that help make up atoms and which have certain distinct and supposedly unchangeable properties, might just be subject to change. Anything on that level might be subject to change, electromagnetic fields, the mass of various particles, or even other attributes of them might alter when hitting one of these kinks.

The particles might be subject to local changes in spacetime. What we thought of as universal constants, those fundamental properties that we think of as being always the same and never changing might just do that—change! This is an incredible idea.

As an example, think of a ping-pong ball floating down a river with a strong current. It behaves a certain way, flows at a certain rate, and due to buoyancy, has a certain amount of itself showing above the waterline. Nevertheless, if it hits a strong eddy or vortex (whirlpool) it could suddenly start spinning in a circle, even changing its direction of flow for a while. The ball could bounce higher out of the water or even temporarily submerge under the force of the eddy or flow of the current in the whirlpool. Particles might behave in a similar sort of fashion when they hit one of these "kinks" or cracks in the quantum field.

If researcher Derevianko and his colleagues are correct in this theory, then (and here we come to how it might affect time again), then our oh-so-accurate satellite clocks might be affected, too. They could become a fraction or so off because of such kinks. In other words, time might change!

How can we use our clocks to determine if this is true? Well, our satellites form a huge circle in space around our globe. This circle, 157,080 kilometers in circumference, is massive and it is moving through the galaxy along with our planet, the other planets in our solar system, and our sun. This makes for a huge and fast moving detection system, since our solar system is orbiting the galaxy at around 15,000 miles per hour.

Now those numbers aside, this just means is that if and/or when our satellite network directly crosses the path of a kink in the quantum fields in space as theorized, it should take no more than 170 seconds for such a kink to travel across the network, or detection system, as we would be using it.

This is of particular significance; because it makes for a great "signature" of such an event, shows us we have crossed such a kink, since other factors disrupting the clocks would not have that same signature.

What does this mean for dark matter? Well, if the theory is correct and proven so by using the GPS satellite system to detect the kinks, we could then next look at pulsars. Pulsars are just the remains of a star that has gone nova (exploded). These pulsars spin at incredible speeds and emit a "pulse" of radiation every time they do. This pulsing is even far more accurate than our GPS satellite clocks. However, every now and then, for some unknown reason, there are trembles in these stars, which scientists refer to as "pulsar quakes." Up until now, we have had no idea what could cause them, although there have been many theories.

One researcher at the University of South Wales, Australia, Victor Flambaum, has come up with the theory that dark matter might be the cause of such quakes. When such a clump of dark matter passes through a pulsar, it might alter the star's structure enough to cause a trembling or pulsar quake. If this is so, then dark matter may actually be such cosmic kinks in the quantum field, rather than some exotic form of unknown matter at all.

If this theory of cosmic kinks proves correct, then it also means the constants of the universe change when things pass through these kinks.

This would provide real proof that reality can fundamentally alter within our universe, as the properties of particles (and we are made up of them), are altered by passing through these cracks in the quantum field.

Furthermore, since time behaves very strangely already on the quantum scale, and quantum effects can occur on the macro scale in some instances, as we now know, then time, itself, might alter, as well. Put simply, if reality can change, then time must be subject to such changes, too, since it makes up a big part of our reality, as we know it. In addition, if time can change in this fashion, it means than there is nothing absolute about it, as we once thought, but instead time is something malleable and able to be "shifted." If time shifts, then this means it is subject to manipulation, as in time travel.

**Conclusion:** Possible kinks in the fabric of spacetime could well be "cracks" in our universe. Moreover, space isn't just space alone. Einstein coined the term "spacetime," because he proved with his theories that the two, space and time, are a sort of manifestation of each other, bound up together as one. So if there are cracks in the one, space, then there are cracks in the other…time, as well.

The intriguing and yes, rather frightening idea is that when Earth and the rest of our solar system passes through one of these kinks or cracks, can people then be more prone to "falling" through such cracks in spacetime? Are there special moments when this can be more likely to happen?

If we judge by all the stories that we've heard of people seeing the future, the past, and even entering both different times, as well as alternate realities, this could well be the explanation for such events. These cracks wouldn't just be in the matter of our universe, but in time, itself, as well. So, "falling through the cracks" might just be what happens to some people and sometimes, with disastrous results for them, because they may not come back out of such cracks in our reality, but end up somewhere, or "somewhen" else entirely. A chilling thought…

# CHAPTER 20

# Black-Eyed Children Time Travelers?

*"According to 'M' theory, ours is not the only universe. Instead, 'M' theory predicts that a great many universes were created out of nothing."*

— Stephen Hawking

Not so long ago there was a radio show on George Noory's Coast-To-Coast AM that raised an interesting subject. The topic concerned the matter of time, or more specifically, timelines and a rather strange thing associated with them. This is the subject known to the world of the paranormal as "the Black-Eyed Children." These children, seen by many, have coal-black eyes. They are featureless ones that do not gleam or seem like human eyes in any way, according to those who have interacted with them. In fact, except for the fact they aren't almond shaped, these children's' eyes fit the classic description of those most famous of UFO aliens, "the grays."

What do these Black-Eyed Children have to do with time travel? Well, according to what a call-in person said there might be a connection and in an intimate way. The caller insisted that such Black-Eyed Children were forcing him to time travel, and not just once, but repeatedly.

Moreover, every time he had to do this, he felt as if he was "losing a piece" of his soul, as he put it. He does not claim they will harm a person in the ordinary sense, but rather are soul stealers of some sort, somehow taking, bit by bit, the essence of the person. The caller felt this was in a spiritual sense.

Furthermore, he claimed the children made him travel through time against his will and desire. His claim was they had sent him forward in time, several centuries, and then back again and did this repeatedly. In the process, he feels he has become *"lost to time."* He can no longer remember anything about his own family and this no matter how hard he tries.

He's not the only one who claims the Black-Eyed Children have some relationship to time travel. In an article in a magazine (*Mysterious Universe*) published on this subject in 2013, it stated another person claimed the children were not of this time. In this case, the person described the children as being dressed as if from another time period, the 1980s, and very much so in detail, wearing items of clothing no longer now available. He said it was as if they had somehow missed what they should have been wearing for the current time. Alternatively, he said that perhaps those were their original clothing and so maybe, they had come from the 1980's.

Just who are the Black-Eyed Children? Well, many often refer to them as an "urban legend." The first reports of them, seem to have come from a man by the name of Brian Bethel, who referenced them on an Internet mailing list he had done, one about all things "ghost."

Black-Eyed Children or "kids" as he called them, were mentioned on a number of occasions in these mailing lists, along with several accounts about them. However, since there are a number of reports by independent witnesses at different times and locations, it's hard to imagine there isn't some basis in reality for the idea of these children, or something very like them, actually existing.

The one thing that stands out with these stories is the terror involved. Everyone who experiences the Black-Eyed Children appears to suffer extreme terror, either during or after the encounter. The initial encounters took place in Texas, as well as Oregon. After that, others began relating their experiences and the Black-Eyed Children quickly became an Internet phenomenon. Mr. Bethel even appeared on television, on the television show, *Monster and Mysteries In America*. After this, the stories of Mr. Bethel, and now others, as well, began to spread ever wider.

The tales of Black-Eyed Children even went worldwide. The *Daily Star* newspaper in England ran a trilogy of front-page articles on the children and even tied them in with a Staffordshire pub (an inn or tavern), one supposedly haunted. As a Wikipedia article on the subject said:

*"The paper claimed a "shock rise in sightings around the world".[8] Alleged sightings are taken seriously by ghost hunters, some of whom believe black eyed children to be extraterrestrials, vampires, or ghosts."*

These stories of Black-Eyed Children closely resemble, as Wikipedia also mentions by referencing Sharon A. Hill, a science writer, that:

*"...the legend of "black eyed kids resembles typical spooky folklore stories in the same realm as phantom black dogs, apparitions, and mysterious monsters...."*

So are Black-Eyed Children real? Well, there are tales of repeated involvement with them by unsuspecting people. They also seem to appear to people as if from out of nowhere. Often, they act as if they are in some sort of trouble and request help from their intended victim. Other times, they instead offer help to people. If one does accept their help, or tries to offer aid to them at their request, the results are not just strange, but downright bizarre.

For example, again with the caller on the radio show, he claims he became a victim of a seesaw-like swinging through time, with each passing back and forth over the centuries slowly draining him of all memory of his personal life, or "soul," as he put it.

Nor is he alone in this. Others claim, and in some cases even have witnesses to events that seem to involve time travel after abduction in some way by these children. Always, the story is the same. People taken against their will and somehow, they travel through time. In the process, they suffer great personal trauma.

**Conclusion.** These tales of the Black-Eyed Children and their forcibly causing people to time travel abound, but it is hard to discern the truth of them, whether they are hoaxes or not, on the one hand, and/or just urban legends.

On the other hand, is there something more to them? There is the fact that some people seem convinced these things really happened to them. Moreover, the tales are remarkably consistent and frightening in their aspects from story to story.

This consistency is a telling point for me, for it means that either people are in collusion, or they are telling the truth as they see it. Furthermore, collusion by total strangers from around the world hardly seems likely or realistic.

So are Black-Eyed Children just an Internet myth? Again, it's hard to say. However, the stories of disappearing and reappearing people, are many, and so are a social phenomenon in their own right. In addition, if true, then we are dealing with a very strange and perhaps dangerous thing, indeed.

Finally, the questions arise, if the Black-Eyed Children are real, then who are they? From where or when are they are? What are they doing here? In addition, the most important question of all, perhaps, what do they want? Maybe, someday, we will find out and unfortunately, we may not like the answer to this last question. The overwhelming terror the victims endure in these tales does not bode well for the idea the Black-Eyed Children are benevolent or kind beings.

# CHAPTER 21
# Time Storms?

*"Time flies over us, but leaves its shadow behind."*

—Nathaniel Hawthorne

There is also the phenomenon of time storms. The pilot, Bruce Gernon in Florida, and perhaps Mr. Goddard in Great Britain, both mentioned near the beginning of this book, might have been victims of just such a thing. They might have entered some type of vortex in the clouds or otherwise (as Mr. Gernon claims), and so passed through a time storm of sorts. Sometimes, inadvertent time travelers such as they seem to have been, ended up back in their own time after it was all over, as if nothing were amiss, but only after having glimpsed the future or past.

Other times, as with Bruce Gernon and his father, they experienced a jump through time and in that case, space, as well. This could well be, since as mentioned earlier, even Einstein believed space and time were bound together. Moreover, Mr. Gernon and Sir Goddard are not alone in this phenomenon. There are other examples of these so-called time storms, as author, Jenny Randles relates in her book, *Time Storms*. She speaks of a number of cases of these strange alterations in time for individuals involved in such time storms, and some are of particular interest here. For example:

**A Disappearing Host.** In England, a man by the name of Peter Williamson decided to have a barbecue. A storm approached, lightning flashed, and thunder crashed. His pet dog, frightened by the uproar of the violent storm, fled to shelter under a tree. Mr. Williamson went to the trembling canine's aid, but as he approached the animal, there was another lightning strike, very close this time.

Mr. Williamson disappeared. With the vision of the guests at last cleared from the brilliant burst of light, they searched for, but could not find him. In desperation, they eventually summoned the authorities. The police, too, were unable to locate Peter's whereabouts, despite a thorough search of the whole area.

However, one morning, and some three days later, they discovered Peter at the edge of a nearby pond. He half stood in the water, half in some shrubs edging the pond. To the onlookers, he had all the appearance of someone who had just materialized out of thin air at that moment. He had no recollection of what had happened during the intervening time, either. Indeed, he wasn't aware there had been any intervening time since his disappearance!

**A Disappearing Soldier.** In April of 1977, in Putre, Chile, a soldier made reports of strange lights. He said the lights, a light violet in color, were moving toward the troops' current positions. The Chilean soldiers were in the midst of a training program when this occurred.

It was early in the morning, still dark when one soldier, a corporal, went to find out just what the lights were or meant. Then a bizarre thing happened. No more than a quarter of an hour later, he returned, but not from the direction that he had taken. Instead, he came from the opposite one. He was in some kind of trance, almost as if sleepwalking, or so his fellow soldiers claimed. He distinctly said:

*"You do not know who we are or where we come from."*

The truly strange thing was that although he had only been gone a matter of fifteen minutes or so, he was said to now bear the equivalent growth of about a week's worth of beard. He had set out on April 24. However, upon his return, his watch displayed the date as April 30. By these measures, he seemed to have been gone about a week. Yet by everyone else's measure of time, he had only been gone a quarter of an hour! Nor could he account for his whereabouts during that time, whether the fifteen minutes or the week.

**Translocation of Vehicles.** In 1981, a business representative, Jorge Ramos, drove his Volkswagen from his home to attend a meeting nearby. However, when he failed to appear, the others there were surprised, because he was usually very good about punctuality, and never missed such meetings. Concerned as more time went by, they raised the alarm.

Later, although his car was located, of Jorge, there was no sign. The vehicle was off one side of the highway when discovered. Apparently, Jorge or someone parked it there. Some five days passed without any sign of the man. Then, his wife received a telephone call from him. His explanation was that he had been heading to the meeting just as he usually did. Everything was normal until suddenly he encountered a bizarre area of light that enveloped him and his vehicle. He felt cut off, as if in a trance.

When he recovered, he found himself just standing alone alongside a different road than the one he had been traveling on in his car. He quickly realized days had passed and was over half a thousand miles from where the white light had enveloped him.

Mr. Ramos could not account for this translocation in not only space, but time, as well. This is not the only such instance of people translocating while in their vehicles, as we have seen, as with the pilots in both the United Kingdom and Florida, along with many others.

Also according to Ms. Randles' book, in Maine, a man by the Name of David Stephens and a companion, were in his car. This was in a rural, wooded area. They had heard an odd noise not far away and so had decided to track it down.

However, as they approached an area in their vehicle where they thought might have been the source of the noise, they, too, experienced a strange brilliance surrounding them. Then, they realized they were close to a mile from where they just had been and their vehicle now faced the other way around. How this had occurred, they couldn't say, for they had no recollection. The account also goes on to say they also later endured strange afflictions, physical and mental ones, as well. Therefore, there seems to have been lasting repercussions in this instance of translocation.

However, is there any other evidence to corroborate MS Randles' time storm idea? Yes, there seems to be some, at least. For example, in 1996, a security camera at a factory in Florida recorded a truly strange phenomenon.

As a factory employee moved toward one of the monitored gates on camera, another one of those weird glows of white light blanked out all sight of the man. At this point, the camera suffered an electronic disruption of its recording, but in seconds, the interference had passed. The camera then functioned again. However, now, there was no sign of the worker.

Yet, just under two hours later, the man flashed back onto the image, now on his hands and knees and vomiting. Additionally, he couldn't account for his two-hour disappearance, had no memory of it at all. Since all this was on videotape, it does add real credence to the idea of these mysterious white glows enveloping something or someone, and then the person and/or vehicle translocating in time, or even time and space combined. For more on this topic, please see the link to MS Randles' book under *"References."*

**Conclusion:** Although many stories of people disappearing for good, or reappearing days later, often in different locations, all seem anecdotal only, they are not. In most if not quite all the cases where this sort of thing seems to have taken place, there are witnesses to the events, worried family members and friends, as well as acquaintances and business associates involved.

For instance, to say that a group of people witnessed their host vanish before their eyes in a bright flash of lightning, only to be found several days later nearby with no idea of what had happened to him is a hoax, seems unlikely. This is especially so, since police were involved. The guests at the barbeque were a variety of people, some close to their host, others little more than acquaintances.

How could so many disparate persons, all having different and varying relationships with their host be involved in such a pointless hoax? Where was the advantage, the payoff? There was none, and to arrange for a flash of lightning to occur on demand seems a ludicrous idea, at best. Likewise, again, they had called the police. In England, wasting police time is a very serious offense, so few would do such a thing lightly. Nor could the authorities, despite scouring the home and entire area, find the man until he simply reappeared.

Furthermore, the stories of such events are hardly limited to the ones included here in this book. There are far more of them than would be practical to include. Besides, as with one of the above tales, there had been videotape recordings to back up the story. In fact, the video tape was the source of the story (that, and the factory worker himself). So some of the anecdotes related, at the very least, seem genuine.

In addition, one must remember that soldiers are subject to strict military discipline. For a group of them to aid a fellow soldier in such a hoax, to directly disobey orders, and then to outright lie to their commanders about it, just doesn't seem too likely a thing to have happened. Far more likely, they all told the truth as they saw it, at least. Besides which, one of those in charge saw the strange lights, so there is corroboration in that regard, too.

Are there time storms in our skies, on our seas, and land, as well? Do they envelop the odd person or persons and sometime their vehicles, too? Well, something certainly seems to be doing this, because these stories date back centuries! Therefore, if they are all hoaxes in their multitudes, it is a very old sort of hoax, indeed.

More likely, "something" is actually happening to many people. Whether this "something" is a time storm, is uncertain. Still, given the descriptions and evidence, it would seem to be one of the most plausible explanations to date.

# CHAPTER 22

## A Caveat — Beware of Hoaxes

*In a secular age, an authentic miracle must purport to be a hoax, in order to gain credit in the world.*

— Angela Carter

With regard to some of the uncertainty of anecdotal tales related here in this book, there must be a caveat mentioned. Whenever dealing with any of these more otherworldly subjects, it is important always to keep a somewhat skeptical mind, as well as having an open one. The two should go hand in hand. There are hoaxers out there, and the Internet seems to be one of their favorite places to play, so always double and triple-check such things, such tales, before even beginning to entertain the idea they might just be true.

However, the Internet is hardly the only place where hoaxes are perpetrated on the unsuspecting. Whether the authorities, businesses, private citizens, or any type of organization, including corporate ones, all can become the victims of such practical jokes and the charlatans who perpetrate them.

Time travel tales have the same problem. There are people creating hoaxes on a regular basis, and some of these are about time travel.

In addition, as camera-editing capabilities steadily improve, for still photographs and videos, it gets harder and harder with each passing year to determine what is "real" and what isn't.

Following, is just one example, one of many of just this sort of thing, stories that received wide publicity, had many people believing in them, only then later, after the fact, considered more likely as a hoax:

In 2003, this story (see image below) appeared in the newspapers. A man by the name of Andrew Carlssin, who was something of a "whiz," on Wall Street, as one article put it, was arrested. Later released on bail, he broke the terms of his release by disappearing.

Now, this would be just another "insider-trading" story, one of many we have heard of in these troubled economic times. However, this one is a little different, in that Andrew Carlssin made the astonishing claim he was from the year 2256.

Carlssin, 44 years old, used this as his reason for being able to make so much money on the stock exchange so quickly, because he knew what stocks were going to go up and down before they actually did! This is allegedly according to the SEC (Security and Exchange Commission).

He supposedly gave this explanation at the time of his initial arrest. The SEC did not buy this story at all, and one can see why. Still, the man managed to turn a mere $800 into $350 million in just two weeks' time! So obviously, he must have known something from some source. The SEC felt this was due to "insider trading." In short, he was getting knowledge illegally of what was going on with some stocks and companies.

A series of seemingly high-risk trades alerted agents of the SEC to the idea that Carlssin might be doing something illegal. When he was taken in for questioning, they listened to a four-hour confession, one in which he consistently insisted he was a time traveler. He made many claims about this aspect of things. He said our period, in the future, had a thorough and detailed history, as one that had suffered serious economic upheavals. He acquired this detailed information, which he then utilized to come back in time and make his money.

At the time of his confession, now some years ago, he offered as a plea bargain the cure for AIDS, as well as the then-current location of Osama Bin Laden. In payment, he just wanted to return to his time traveling vehicle and then journey back to his own time, some two hundred years into our future. The location of this vehicle, he would never tell.

After his bail release, he disappeared, never to be seen again, at least so far... Furthermore, the authorities say they have no record of an "Andrew Carlssin" ever having existed prior to the time of their inquiries into him.

All this sounds very convincing, doesn't it? So many intricate details mentioned, what with the SEC, his arrest, etc. A man appears, makes a fortune in two weeks, and then jumps bail and disappears back through time...maybe.

However, As Wikipedia states about the Weekly World News, the newspaper is a: *"largely fictional news tabloid."*

As compelling as the article originally seemed to be, it doesn't now sound as if it rings quite so truthfully, does it? A hoax? It could well be, and very probably is. Certainly, Mr. Andrew Carlssin having ever really existed seems unlikely now, at the very least.

This is just one example of many hoaxes perpetrated along these lines. At first blush, they seem real enough, very detailed and convincing to the readers, but once one considers the source of each of them, this might make them then seem highly suspect in nature, as this story definitely does. One can't say for sure if it is a hoax, but one can surely entertain the idea with a reasonable degree of credibility that it is.

**Supposed Newspaper Account.**

Therefore, one must take such stories with a very large grain of salt and be willing to do a little fact checking to make sure the tale of time travel holds up under at least some reasonable scrutiny. In this case, it simply does not.

Yes, there is still some room for doubt. Tabloids do often distort things, make up things, but they also tell the truth sometimes, as well. I leave it to the reader to decide if they think this was a real event, or just another hoax perpetrated by the tabloid in question. In my opinion, because I can find no alternate sources, I must conclude it is most likely a hoax.

**Another Hoaxer.** John Titor was a self-proclaimed time traveler who said he was from the year 2036, not really so very far from now. Furthermore, being from the future, he made quite a number of predictions. Among his many claims was the time he lived in, the America of that supposed future, was not really one, but rather five different versions, or regions loosely bound together. Of course, the fact that certain geographers have already broken America down into such cultural regions (as with Northern New England and Maritime Provinces of Canada being one, the Southwest Border States and Mexico being another, etc.,) is a rather telling "coincidence," in and of itself. Did he utilize their information to base his story on?

John Titor said our country was the victim of nuclear strikes and these had done much damage to not only the environment, but the infrastructure of our country, as well. Yet, we still apparently developed time travel about that time, and despite these enormous technological setbacks?

These predictions of John Titor and many others don't seem to be coming true, either, because since his supposed arrival in the early 2000's (although he is a hard man to find or meet, apparently, because nobody has. They just read his postings on the Internet), none of his prophecies have so far come to fruition.

Therefore, we can only assume, and I think rightfully so, that John Titor was just one of many Internet hoaxes, and perhaps one of the first such, since at the time, the Internet was still in its relative infancy. However, as for John Titor being a real time traveler, well…that's just extremely doubtful.

**Philadelphia Experiment.** This famous tale of a ship in the 1940's during World War II transporting through time and space because of a failed government experiment to make it invisible has long withstood the test of time for believability. There have even been a couple of movies made about the supposed event. Additionally, many still believe the tale is true and the truth is that we still can't be at all certain that it isn't.

Even so, the account of the naval vessel, *Eldridge*, popping in and out of existence, and having crew members killed in the process, could well just be a hoax. Why do I say this? For the following reasons:

1. Nobody can confirm the ship was where it was supposed to have been and/or gone to, as stated in the tale. In fact, logs show the ship wasn't in the claimed locations at the times mentioned. Of course, people can forge logs. However,

2. None of the surviving affected crewmembers has ever come forward to bolster the story's veracity in any way and there were many crewmembers on the *Eldridge*.

3. Nor has anyone been able to find any records of any dead crewmembers who supposedly died aboard the *Eldridge* during the time of the experiment.

Again, records can be altered, forged, and whatever, and it seems in some cases, the government is quite capable of such duplicity. Nevertheless, the fact is, there is no real supporting evidence whatsoever to support the story of the *Eldridge* having passed in and out of time and space, or translocating in any way.

It is a tantalizing tale. Even so, the whole thing seems to have little or nothing to back it up in any significant way. Yet, there was an actual *Eldridge,* so again, we can't be sure this was a hoax.

**Fictional Stories Becoming Real.** One also has to be aware of fictional stories that then somehow cross over into being true, or at least, considered so by many. For instance, there is the story of a man dressed in pre-Twentieth Century clothing (1800s) who somehow traveled through time to New York, to the year 1950. When struck by an automobile there, since he was unfamiliar with such vehicles and the dangers they represented to unsuspecting pedestrians, he died. Subsequently, the police examined him and his belonging, only to find his clothes were way behind the current times, and his personal possessions were equally wrong for 1950. They concluded he had accidentally transported through time.

So powerful was this story that as time passed, it spread. This started in the early 1970s and people often quoted it as a real account of an actual event, and as an example of time travel, however inadvertently accomplished. Still, despite the widespread belief this was a true tale, it wasn't.

The anecdote was pure fiction and from a short story titled *"I'm Scared,"* by the author, Jack Finney, who wrote the tale in 1951. The hero of his story, Rudolph Fentz, died just as the supposedly "true account" described.

**Conclusion:** This last example wasn't a deliberate hoax. However, the story, and that's all it was, a fictional tale, became an urban legend very quickly and so through this process passed from fiction to fact. The same thing often occurs with deliberate hoaxes in the same way.

Consequently, it is only with a good deal of caution that anyone interested in the subject of time travel should approach the subject. Make sure to do this in a practical way and with a somewhat skeptical eye, as well.

Does time travel seem to exist despite these hoaxes? Yes, based on the evidence from many sources, it does seem to, or at least, something seems definitely to be going on in that regard. Time travel is real, I think, but it is important always to be careful when examining evidence regarding it, even so.

# CHAPTER 23

# Time Can Flow Backwards?

*"Once confined to fantasy and science fiction, time travel is now simply an engineering problem."*

—Michio Kaku

Time, as we have seen, is hardly the static thing we once thought. As shown so far in this book, time is not only fluid, but we have already begun to deal with that fluidity, actually have to do this when it comes to maintaining our worldwide GPS systems, both ours and the new European one coming online.

There is even more to consider with regard to time and time travel. That is, time might actually be able to run backwards and do this "naturally," if one can use such a description for something so weird.

The first way time might be flowing backwards is in a parallel universe or other universes. When the Big Bang occurred, according to the main and current theories, it is highly likely multiple universes formed, as well, and when I say multiple, I mean multiple! We are talking on an order of, if not precisely infinite (depending on which theory one goes by), then very close to that.

This means there is a VERY good chance of some of the "pocket universes," as they have been called, having different directions in their time flow. Some would flow forward, some would flow backward, and some might even flow "sideways" compared to ours.

Others would flow in these ways, but at different speeds from ours. This is rather mindboggling to consider, no doubt, but the likelihood of this being so is very high according to some cosmologists and physicists, given the number of other universes there could be and should be, based on our current theories of the universe. What this means is that an adjacent universe to us might have its time flowing in reverse to ours. In other words, by our perceptions, time would be moving backwards.

No, this does not mean that everyone there is leaping out of their graves, then growing younger, and then ending back up in their mother's womb before disappearing entirely. It just means their "arrow of time" points in the opposite direction from ours. For anyone in that universe, everything seems normal enough, but it's just that their time is flowing backward, if only compared to ours.

Think of the following analogy: you have two trains traveling on parallel tracks, but in opposite directions. Both trains are moving "forward" from the point of view of everyone on their train, but for the people on the other and passing train, they are going in the reverse direction from their own. For each train then, the passengers see the other train and its passengers as going the opposite way.

For time travel, this means if we could cross over into a parallel universe with a reverse time flow to ours, like crossing over from one of those trains to the other, and then later manage to cross back again before the trains had finished passing by each other, we would end up at some time in our own past!

In other words, to continue using this analogy, we would come again to our train, but further back on it. It's an amazing idea, but perhaps a very real one, according to cosmologists and some physicists.

Another strange phenomenon might also be in play in such a situation. In our train scenario, if you crossed over to the train moving in the reverse direction (an identical parallel universe in this case, but just moving in time opposite to our own), you might board it in its "future," because to continue with our analogy, the trains might not have been perfectly aligned when you made the crossing between them.

Therefore, you might cross over (again, to continue the analogy) from the rear of our train, just as the "front" of the other train is going by. Then you would be in that universe's future compared to where you are in time in ours. The same might also work the other way, if you crossed over from the front of our train/universe to the rear of the other one as it passed.

Then you would be in that universe's far past. In other words, you would be time traveling to different points in that parallel universe, but also again, when you "crossed" back to different times in ours. The future of that universe would be the past of own universe and vice versa. Once more, this might sound like pure science fiction, but if crossing between universes ever turns out to be possible, and some say it could well be, this is just what we might find when we make such a crossing.

Physicists say this sort of thing could also happen if some parallel universes developed more slowly than ours had developed, had a "later start," but were otherwise identical. In which case, we would cross over into what would be our past in that universe.

The reverse would be true, as well. We could conceivably cross over into what would be the future of our universe, if we crossed into one that developed more quickly than ours was doing.

We would see how events yet to unfold in our universe had already turned out in the parallel one.

Is this possible, to have universes with different speeds and directions in their rate of the flow of time? Well, according to Einstein and those annoying GPS locations systems orbiting our Earth, it's already happening in our universe. Time, again as Einstein makes very clear and science has proven repeatedly to be true, is relative.

In this universe, rate of time flow is determined by an object's speed and/or how deep in a gravity well (such as Earth), one might be. So yes, other universes could not only be flowing forward and backward in time with regard to ours, but at different rates of speed. Again, this would be analogous to those two trains traveling in opposite directions to each other, and at different rates of speed.

As for universes going "sideways in time" to ours, the outcome would be different. We would cross over to such a universe, could spend a great deal of time there and then cross back to find we came back to the exact same point in time we'd left.

This would be another form of time traveling. It is a way of spending time elsewhere, perhaps even growing old there, and then coming back to the same "present" one had left. This, too, seems very bizarre, but according to many physicists, it is entirely possible and some say even probable.

**Time Might Move Backward In A Parallel Universe But All Else Stays The Same.**

# CONCLUSION

We have discussed many things here in this book. We have gone over the idea of whether time travel is even possible or not (it seems it certainly is. We've seen sample case histories of those convinced they have time traveled, and we have explored and discussed the idea of time machines and the fact some are already being experimented with to see if they might work. Moreover, there is tantalizing evidence some might already exist, as with the case of Sid Hurwich. Furthermore, we have people claiming some have time traveled, as with Mr. Basiago as a child. Then there are those Black-Eyed Children to consider, as well, and so much more.

In addition, if time travel is possible and a time machine or machines exists right now, here in the present, even if still in the design state, and/or being built, then it could well be true in some future time, as well. Very likely, it would be in all probability.

Furthermore, we've also seen examples of anachronisms repeatedly found in our own historical timeline, things found in archaeological digs and elsewhere that just shouldn't be, shouldn't belong where they were found, if our idea of our history is even marginally correct as it now stands. Numerous items surface all the time from below ground. These include twenty-five-million-year-old ladles and hand bells, (perhaps even older). Archaeologists and laypeople alike, find such things in coal deposits, as well as such items as skeletons embedded in ancient limestone.

Nor does the whole question of time travel end there, because people seemingly switch from one timeline to another, and sometimes with disastrous consequences, as in the Lerina Garcia case. All these cases are examples of the premise that time travel is not only possible, but appears to have happened. Moreover, it seems to happen if not often, then at least on regular occasions.

It doesn't stop there. We have video recordings, as well as sworn testimonies of people who have vanished without a trace, and other people we can't account for (still being "disappeared") to also back up the idea of time travel.

What's more, time travel doesn't just seem to be in a linear fashion, moving forward into the future, or backward in time. It seems we can go sideways in time, as well, to other timelines. As with the reported cases of people just vanishing, some never to return, or others returning (by their time) days later, while only minutes have passed for the rest of us, things with regard to time hardly seem firm and fixed at all. Quite the opposite seems to be the reality.

Cases involving people who either seem to have traveled to the far future, or to timelines so different from ours as to be unrecognizable to the travelers, are also, if not frequent still happening. Furthermore, there are some scientists who insist such travel may be common, that all of us might be shifting to parallel timelines and perhaps back again all the time! Again, as with Lerina, or those young women in Utah, this can have a tremendous impact on their lives, but for most of us, we don't even seem to notice, because the difference between the timelines can be so minor.

Is time as fluid as I contend it to be here in this book? Well, if synchronicities are anything to go by, time is hardly a fixed and reliable thing. It is fluid. My own synchronicity of having experienced a detailed trip through England's west country, only to then see it the very night of our return on television, but that trip having taken place a century ago, is an oddity, no doubt. I don't think I would ever be able rationally or adequately to explain otherwise how this could have occurred.

Time was involved in that synchronicity, of this, I'm sure. The past and the present conjoined in an incredibly "timely" and remarkable way with three of us as witnesses to the event. Nor was this the only synchronicity I've experienced. Moreover, many, many others have experienced these, as well, perhaps in the millions or even more. Again, this happens to so many people so often that Carl Jung, the famous founder, along with Sigmund Freud, of psychology, coined the term "synchronicity" just to describe such bizarre coincidences. Likewise, there are numerous books on the subject, as well. Publishing of such books continues even now.

Besides this, we've seen here that researchers actually discuss, design, and some even attempt building them. We've also seen that there might well have been such devices already made, as with Sid Hurwich's time-freezing device. Additionally, we've had numerous and strange disappearances of persons, with then some even stranger reappearances of such people, and often with weird time discrepancies involved, as for how much time passed for the disappeared versus those who did not. Time travel is a huge subject, a broad one, as we've seen.

**Remember, what we've covered here:**
- Time travel is possible.

- Case histories of time travel, both into the past, as well as into the future.
- Time machines and ways to time travel now being developed and experimented with.
- Time traveler intervention in our past and evidence for this fact.
- People disappearing and reappearing...although not all coming back, and often with time discrepancies involved.
- The Mandela Effect and the possibility of parallel realities, ones which some of us still "remember."
- Alternate timelines.
- The Rendlesham Forest Incident and the belief by the key figure in that event that the ship was from over 6,000 years in the future.
- Binary code algorithms of the same type as used for self-correction of data transmission and the fact these are embedded in the very formulas describing our universe and the possible (probable?) consequences of this discovery for time travel. If we were just a matrix, then time travel would be a way for "someone" to move about in the "game."
- The scientific probability (a high one) we are in such a simulation.
- Glitches in the fabric of our reality, such as synchronicities, and glitches in our timeline. These show reality and time are not the hard and fast things we once thought, but are subject to weird twists, kinks, loops, and bypasses.
- Quantum physics and the fact it may affect us directly on the macroscopic or large scale and not just the super small. Hard scientific evidence now seems to show this. If so, than another phenomenon of the quantum world, the nonlocality of particles in space and time could then affect us, as people, as well. We might experience episodes of

nonlocality of time on our scale, and so be "transported" through time and/or spacetime.

• Black-eyed children and what they might represent for time traveling, since people claim these children cause them to travel into the future and the past, in a "seesaw" type of shifting.

• The fact some physicists claim time doesn't just necessarily move forward or backward, but might well go sideways, as well.

• Chrononauts, people who claim to have been part of a government-funded project to travel through space and time.

• Interference in our history by time travelers with recorded historical events.

**There was much more here in this book, of course, and it all seems to add up to two compelling conclusions:**

1. Time travel is real, and

2. Time travel has already happened, or will have already happened in the future, and that the past has been already visited.

Now, of course, the question arises as to why this is happening. If time travel is real, as many physicists believe it just might be, and if the evidence here does indicate time travel has already happened, then why is it happening? What is the purpose of "others" time traveling.

Well there are a number of reasons why this might be so:

1. Time travelers are just "tourists," as Stephen Hawking put it. They want to just see different times and experience them even as tourists do by traveling the world today.

2. Time travelers are researchers into the past. These researchers are gathering data about our times and other past times, as historians of the future.

3. Time travelers are really those "others" who wish to move around in a simulation of the past, meaning our universe is really a matrix or game. They would do this for whatever reasons they might have, including being gamers or tourists after a fashion, or whatever. If aliens or post-humans, it might not be possible for us "mere" humans to ever understand their true motivations.

4. Time travelers are interfering in our timeline to change events and outcomes for a purpose or purposes unknown. Perhaps the their time didn't turn out the way they wished it to, but with the aid of time traveling devices, they can alter this and create a better "present" for themselves, or even just speed up our advancement by such direct interference.

5. Our universe is a sort of computer game and time travelers are just human descendants acting as players in it. Therefore, time travel would be a way to move around within the different time settings of the game, even as games can move around in different scenarios in today's computer games.

6. Reality isn't at all what we think it is at all, and time travelers are "others" who already know this and so use it to "walk amongst us," in a manner of speaking. Again, the purposes of them doing this are unknown and might just remain so, if this is true, because these "others" might be so alien in concept and behavior, as never to be able for us to be know why they wish to do this.

This last point, Number 6, is not as strange as one might think. Trying to know a truly alien mind might simply be impossible for us to do. After all, we've been struggling to understand dolphins for decades and still do not. We think they might have a language, but if so, it seems incomprehensible to us. The same holds true for the other great apes besides ourselves. We still aren't even sure if they are conscious in the same way that we are, for instance.

Therefore, if "something" from some other reality outside our time and space, and/or even dimension is coming through, we might never be able to understand them. We might not be able to know what they want, what their goals are. Such beings might be able to see the future and past all at once, for instance. Whereas we, like insects trapped in a piece of amber of time, simply cannot. If beings live in other dimensions, this could well be the case if they came to ours.

How would this last be possible? Well, a good analogy might be people living on a mountaintop instead of in a valley. The ones in the valley might never know from one hour to the next what the weather might be like, whereas, the people on the mountaintop, able to see much farther and still quite naturally, could see approaching storms.

If they then went down into the valley to warn the citizens inhabiting there of a bad storm coming, the people they told might think they had special powers, since they could see and foretell something, they, themselves, could not. The same sort of thing might be true of those from other dimensions who came here and in much the same way. We would be astonished if they knew the future, when for them; it might just be a "normal" thing.

Whatever the reason for time travelers, though, one thing seems obvious; if they have already been, and might well be continuing to come into the past, meaning our present, as well as our history and are doing this on purpose, they must have a reason(s). Additionally, I do think they have been doing this and I think the evidence provided here in this book goes a long way towards showing this.

If so, we really should try to learn more about them, because heaven knows, their impact on us could be, and probably has been, profound! How many lives might just have ceased to be altogether because of time changes in our history? The worst part about such an idea is that even worse than dying; those people would never have existed at all.

Remember the case of Lerina Garcia's boyfriend? He was the one she can now find no trace of ever having existed at all. Yet, she still loves and mourn his loss, although as far as can be determined, he never existed at all, at least, not in this timeline. This is exactly what I'm talking about here, and it is a truly frightening idea, that people not only can just cease to be, but then never have been at all. At least, when people die, we have our legitimate memories of them and so can grieve and remember them. However, if they suddenly ceased EVER to have existed at all, could we still do this? Would we even remember they had existed once?

Furthermore, if time is fluid, perhaps just an illusion, then the idea that we can become unstuck in time and even from this universe is also a chilling thought. For the lives of those that we love, and for us personally, this is a great deal, the central reason for our existence — to love and be loved by our partners, wives, husbands, children, parents, friends, etc.

However, what if they are all just some weird illusion of time, and those we love are actually a multitude of such lookalike persons switching back and forth between adjacent parallel worlds, an infinity of them all the time, even as we, ourselves might be doing, too?

If this is so, then just who are those people we think we know and love so well? Do we love them all, or is there one specific one among them that we loved and have already unwittingly lost and don't even realize it?

In other words, as Edgar Allan Poe once said in one of his poems, "A Dream Within A Dream," published in 1849:

*"Is all that we see or seem but a dream within a dream?"*

When it comes to the matter of time and time travel, let us hope this is not how it is, because the implications of such a thing make for a vast, cold, and rather uncaring universe, if so. Still, no matter how we look at time travel, if it is real and I think this books provides ample evidence it probably is, then the implications are still vast, even so.

Whatever their reasons, whether to alter the future, to observe our present and past, to play in some vast computer simulation of which we are just a part, or whatever, the consequences for us are profound. We might simply cease to be at any moment. On the other hand, someone or something (post-human, alien, etc.) might be altering our timeline to bring about a future they want, and not one we might want. Alternatively, if we are just a computer simulation, what's to stop "them" from simply turning the program off and snuffing out all of us in the process?

Time travelers, whether they are for good or ill remains to be seen, but they do seem to have the power to manipulate our timeline, our lives, at will and therefore us. This means we are at their mercy, and the fact is, they may not be of a merciful nature.

This is why we need to know, to search for answers, because the consequences might be too terrible to contemplate. Of course, even if we find the answers, "they" might simply alter the timeline again so we didn't...

Still, one can only try. Therefore, it would behoove us to find out for certain, since the consequences can, and already might have, affected us deeply.

As the proverbial ostrich found out, to bury one's head in the sand, whether the sands of time or otherwise, is no real guarantee of safety. Invaders, whether from "out there," or from some future time, are a potential threat we must learn more about. Otherwise, we risk our very existence, our ever having even existed, for that matter, if we do not. Such a time travel invasion of our timeline, therefore, is definitely not necessarily a good thing, at least, not for those of us who presently exist...

The choice is yours, as a reader, whether to believe the evidence provided here or not. I have simply presented the information available. I have made my opinion clear.

Now, it is up to you to decide for yourselves if time travel is real and if it has happened already. Don't wait too long to reach a decision, though, because who knows, perhaps our "time" is fast running out, as well...

# ABOUT THE AUTHOR

Rob Shelsky is an avid and eclectic writer, and averages about 4,000 words a day. Rob, with a degree in science, has written a large number of factual articles for the former AlienSkin Magazine, as well as for other magazines, such as *Doorways, Midnight Street (U.K.), Internet Review of Science Fiction (IROSF)*, and many others. While at *AlienSkin Magazine*, a resident columnist there for about seven years, Rob did a number of investigative articles, including some concerning the paranormal, as well as columns about UFOs. He conducted interviews of those who have had encounters with them.

He has often and over a long period, explored the Alien and UFO question and has made investigative trips to research such UFO hotspot areas as Pine Bush, New York, Gulf Breeze, Florida, and other such regions, including Brown Mountain, North Carolina, known, for the infamous "Brown Mountain Lights, as well as investigating numerous places known for paranormal activity. He has even traveled overseas in order to do this.

With over 20 years of such research and investigative efforts behind him, Author Rob Shelsky is well qualified in the subject of UFOs, as well as that of the paranormal. Where Rob Shelsky tends to be the skeptic, and insists upon being able to "kick the tires" of a UFO, to ascertain their reality for certain, he is, as well, a theorist, constantly coming up with possible explanations for various such phenomena. Rob asks the hard questions others seem to avoid. Often, he comes up with convincing answers and theories to explain such things.

Currently, Rob lives in North Carolina on two acres in the country. He takes a daily walk to the lake and while doing so, contemplates the nature of the universe. It is from this wellspring of meditation that his idea for various books first seem to surface. After that, as he puts it, it's "just a lot of hard work" to get those ideas researched and written.

For links to other books written, please go to:

http://home.earthlink.net/~robngeorge/

Or: http://robshelsky.blogspot.com/

Or: http://www.amazon.com/gp/search/ref=sr_tc_2_0?rh=i%3Astripbooks%2Ck%3ARob+Shelsky&keywords=Rob+Shelsky&ie=UTF8&qid=1298820526&sr=1-2-ent&field-contributor_id=B002BO9RIE

# REFERENCES

https://en.wikipedia.org/wiki/Speed_of_light Speed of Light, Wikipedia

http://www.physics.org/article-questions.asp?id=131

http://www.astronomy.ohio-state.edu/~pogge/Ast162/Unit5/gps.html

https://en.wikipedia.org/wiki/Speed_of_light

https://en.wikipedia.org/wiki/Casimir_effect for Casimir Effect

https://en.wikipedia.org/wiki/Hawking_radiation for Hawking Radiation and Negative Energy

http://www.strangerdimensions.com/2012/07/17/could-a-kerr-black-hole-be-used-to-travel-through-time/ Kerr Black Holes and Time Travel

http://www.slashfilm.com/wp/wp-content/images/timetravelconcept.jpg Time Travel Loop according to Professor Mallet

https://en.wikipedia.org/wiki/Moberly%E2%80%93Jourdain_incident#cite_note-qtd_Castle_194-13 Versailles Time Travel Incident

Iremonger, Lucille (1975). *The Ghosts of Versailles*: Miss Moberly and Miss Jourdain and their Adventure. White Lion.

Coleman, Michael H (1988). *The Ghosts of the Trianon, The Complete Adventure*. Aquarian Press.

http://www.labyrinthina.com/void.html, *Dimensions Beyond Our Own*, Corrales, Scott

Brennan, JH. *Time Travel: A New Perspective*

http://www.labyrinthina.com/the-bermuda-triangle-fog.html Bruce Gernon, *The Time Vortex*

Begg, Paul (1979). *Into Thin Air: People Who Disappear*

Slemen, Thomas (1998). Strange But True: Mysterious and Bizarre People

https://theghostinmymachine.wordpress.com/2015/07/06/unresolved-who-was-the-man-from-taured-and-did-he-even-exist-at-all/ "Lucia's" blog

http://inexplicata.blogspot.com/, *Inexplicta* blog

http://www.messagetoeagle.com/unexplained-disappearance-of-a-professor-who-perhaps-entered-a-parallel-world/ Vanishing Venezuelan Professor

Swartz, Tim. *Edge of Time*. Bold Street, Liverpool, UK

http://www.educatinghumanity.com/2012/02/time-traveltop-ten-people-who-time.html Liverpool Time Travel Street

https://en.wikipedia.org/wiki/Bold_Street,_Liverpool Liverpool Time Travel

http://www.messagetoeagle.com/threeoldtimetravelcases.php#ixzz3mCbeXBcY Time Travel Incidents

http://www.strangemag.com/highstrangenesstimetrav.html *Strange Magazine* Highway Incident Article

*Time Storms: Amazing Evidence for Time Warps, Space Rifts and Time Travel*, Randle, Jenny

http://www.bloomberg.com/news/articles/2015-03-27/a-physicist-is-building-a-time-machine-to-reconnect-with-his-dead-father Professor Ron Mallet and His Time Machine

http://academicminute.org/2015/02/ron-mallett-uconn-theories-of-time-travel/ Professor Ron Mallet

https://www.google.com/search?q=is+story+of+Sid+Huriwch+a+hoax%3F&ie=utf-8&oe=utf-8 Sid Hurwich and His Time Machine

http://wackulus.com/mystery-sid-hurwich-machine-freeze-time/ Sid Hurwich

http://www.messagetoeagle.com/mystery-of-sid-hurwich-and-his-time-altering-machine-that-could-freeze-time/#ixzz40Llwchtj Sid Hurwich and His Time Machine http://mandelaeffect.com/history-explain-alternate-geographical-memories/ The Mandela Effect

http://mandelaeffect.com/more-moving-countries/ Moving Countries

http://www.vice.com/read/the-berensteain-bears-conspiracy-theory-that-has-convinced-the-internet-there-are-parallel-universes Berenstain Bears Conspiracy Theory

http://www.godlikeproductions.com/forum1/message691708/pg1 Henry VIII With Turkey Leg

http://mandelaeffect.com/henry-viii-portrait-turkey-leg/ Henry VIII With Turkey Leg

Penniston, Jim, *Encounter in Rendlesham Forest*, Thomas Dunne Books; Reprint edition, April 15, 2014

http://www.pbs.org/wgbh/nova/blogs/physics/2015/07/are-we-living-in-a-computer-simulation/ Simulated Universe?

http://theawakenment.com/theoretical-physicist-james-gates-finds-computer-code-in-string-theory-equation/#sthash.OWoBNA3m.dpbs Binary Code In String Theory.

http://education.jlab.org/qa/atomicstructure_10.html Nothing Is "Solid."

http://motherboard.vice.com/read/there-is-growing-evidence-that-our-universe-is-a-giant-hologram Our Universe A Hologram?

http://www.dailymail.co.uk/sciencetech/article-3057957/Are-living-HOLOGRAM-time-scientists-prove-strange-theory-true-realistic-models-universe.html Our Universe a Hologram?

http://www.amazon.com/gp/product/B003PJ6UHA/ref=dp-kindle-redirect?ie=UTF8&btkr=1 Lanza, Robert, *Biocentrism: How Life and Consciousness are the Keys to Understanding the True Nature of the Universe*

Talbot, Michael, *The Holographic Universe*, http://www.amazon.com/The-Holographic-Universe-Revolutionary-Reality/dp/0062014102

http://www.mindpowernews.com/ExploreFutureConsciousness.htm Five Seconds Into The Future

http://kotaku.com/5687716/science-proves-we-can-see-the-future Science Proves We Can See The Future

http://www.mindopenerz.com/your-mind-can-sense-the-future/ Your Mind Can Sense The Future

Quantum Drum, Cleland, http://physicsworld.com/cws/article/news/2010/mar/18/quantum-effect-spotted-in-a-visible-object

http://www.amazon.com/Time-Storms-Jenny-Randles/dp/0425187373 Randles, Jenny, *Time Storm*

https://theghostinmymachine.wordpress.com/2015/07/06/unresolved-who-was-the-man-from-taured-and-did-he-even-exist-at-all/, Randles, Jenny, Statements

http://www.sciencedaily.com/releases/2012/10/121022145342.htm News Summary

http://www.foxnews.com/story/2008/06/03/scientist-humans-can-see-into-future.html Scientists Say We Can See Into The Future

http://www.amazon.com/Deadly-UFOs-And-The-Disappeared-ebook/dp/B00TZ98K9U *Deadly UFOS And The Disappeared*, Shelsky, Rob

https://en.wikipedia.org/wiki/Quantum_entanglement Quantum Entanglement

https://www.sciencerecorder.com/news/2014/11/18/gps-and-atomic-clocks-find-dark-matter/ Dark Matter May Just Be Cosmic Kinks on Quantum Fields

http://www.smh.com.au/technology/sci-tech/time-travel-gods-particle-and-higgs-singlet-how-messages-might-be-sent-to-the-past-or-future-20110322-1c4qq.html The Higgs Singlet

http://www.amazon.com/Mysteries-Of-Time-Travel-Intrusion-ebook/dp/B008IVNKPA *Mysteries Of Time Travel: 35 Cases Of Time Travel Intrusion?* Shelsky, Rob

http://en.wikipedia.org/wiki/Mongol_invasions_of_Japan, China's Invasion of Japan

http://asianhistory.about.com/od/japan/a/Mongolinvasion.htm

http://en.wikipedia.org/wiki/Kamikaze

http://www.historum.com/medieval-byzantine-history/765-divine-wind-destroys-mongol-army.html

http://www.britannica.com/EBchecked/topic/1483622/kamikaze-of-1274-and-1281

http://expertscolumn.com/content/kamikaze-or-divine-wind-saved-japan

http://www.wardsbookofdays.com/29july.htm Spanish Armada

http://www.history.com/topics/weather-in-war

http://www.tudorplace.com.ar/Documents/defeat_of_the_armada.htm

http://www.britainexpress.com/History/tudor/armada.htm

http://uk.answers.yahoo.com/question/index?qid=20120316101333AAHG9Yk

http://en.wikipedia.org/wiki/He_blew_with_His_winds,_and_they_were_scattered "Storm Of Providence" Saves Washington D.C.

http://historicaldigression.com/2012/03/26/a-tornado-saves-washington-during-the-war-of-1812/

http://blogs.smithsonianmag.com/science/2010/08/the-tornado-that-saved-washington/

http://voices.washingtonpost.com/capitalweathergang/2010/07/the_thunderstorm_that_saved_wa.html

**http://www.rense.com/general/utah.htm** Utah's Time/Space Warp Gadianton Canyon Encounter

**https://en.wikipedia.org/wiki/Time_travel_urban_legends**

http://www.livescience.com/28822-sandy-island-undiscovered.html Sandy Island

http://www.brainyquote.com/quotes/keywords/hoax.html

http://www.express.co.uk/news/weird/600855/PICTURED-The-STAGGERING-photos-thought-to-PROVE-time-travel-EXISTS Photos Of Time Travelers?

http://whatculture.com/science/10-compelling-pieces-evidence-prove-alternate-realities-real.php/11

http://www.brainyquote.com/quotes/topics/topic_time.html